50 Vegetarian Mexican Cuisine Recipes for Home

By: Kelly Johnson

Table of Contents

- Vegetarian Tacos
- Black Bean Enchiladas
- Veggie Fajitas
- Chiles Rellenos
- Spinach and Mushroom Quesadillas
- Mexican Street Corn (Elote)
- Vegetarian Tamales
- Stuffed Poblano Peppers
- Sweet Potato and Black Bean Burritos
- Mexican Rice
- Guacamole
- Vegetarian Tortilla Soup
- Roasted Vegetable Tostadas
- Cheese and Bean Pupusas
- Avocado Salad
- Mexican Stuffed Peppers
- Veggie Nachos
- Cilantro Lime Rice
- Refried Beans
- Vegetarian Pozole
- Zucchini and Corn Tacos
- Mexican Quinoa Salad
- Cheese Enchiladas
- Salsa Verde
- Pico de Gallo
- Grilled Veggie Tacos
- Mexican Corn Salad
- Black Bean Soup
- Jalapeño Poppers
- Vegetarian Sopes
- Red Posole
- Spinach Enchiladas
- Veggie Chilaquiles
- Bean and Cheese Taquitos
- Mexican Cauliflower Rice

- Vegetarian Empanadas
- Avocado Tacos
- Lentil Tacos
- Nopalitos Salad
- Veggie Tamale Pie
- Roasted Tomatillo Salsa
- Vegetarian Frito Pie
- Chipotle Sweet Potato Tacos
- Mexican Grilled Corn Salad (Esquites)
- Roasted Pepper Quesadillas
- Mexican Black Bean Salad
- Cauliflower Tacos
- Vegan Taco Salad
- Veggie Stuffed Avocados
- Mexican Chocolate Avocado Mousse

Vegetarian Tacos

Ingredients:

- 1 tablespoon olive oil
- 1 small red onion, diced
- 2 cloves garlic, minced
- 1 bell pepper, diced
- 1 zucchini, diced
- 1 cup corn kernels (fresh or frozen)
- 1 can black beans, drained and rinsed
- 1 teaspoon chili powder
- 1/2 teaspoon cumin
- 1/2 teaspoon smoked paprika
- Salt and pepper to taste
- 8 small corn or flour tortillas
- 1 avocado, sliced
- 1/2 cup cherry tomatoes, halved
- Fresh cilantro, chopped
- Lime wedges
- Crumbled queso fresco or shredded cheese (optional)
- Hot sauce (optional)

Instructions:

1. Heat the olive oil in a large skillet over medium heat.
2. Add the diced red onion and sauté for about 3 minutes until it starts to soften.
3. Add the minced garlic and cook for another minute until fragrant.
4. Add the diced bell pepper and zucchini to the skillet. Sauté for about 5-7 minutes until the vegetables are tender.
5. Stir in the corn kernels and black beans. Cook for an additional 3-4 minutes until heated through.
6. Season the vegetable mixture with chili powder, cumin, smoked paprika, salt, and pepper. Stir well to combine and cook for another 2 minutes.
7. Warm the tortillas in a dry skillet or microwave.
8. Assemble the tacos by spooning the vegetable mixture onto each tortilla.
9. Top with avocado slices, cherry tomatoes, fresh cilantro, and a squeeze of lime juice.
10. If desired, add crumbled queso fresco or shredded cheese and a drizzle of hot sauce.

11. Serve immediately and enjoy your delicious vegetarian tacos!

Black Bean Enchiladas

Ingredients:

- 1 tablespoon olive oil
- 1 small onion, diced
- 2 cloves garlic, minced
- 1 bell pepper, diced
- 1 can black beans, drained and rinsed
- 1 cup corn kernels (fresh or frozen)
- 1 teaspoon ground cumin
- 1 teaspoon chili powder
- 1/2 teaspoon smoked paprika
- Salt and pepper to taste
- 2 cups enchilada sauce (store-bought or homemade)
- 8 small flour or corn tortillas
- 1 1/2 cups shredded cheese (cheddar, Monterey Jack, or a blend)
- Fresh cilantro, chopped (for garnish)
- Sliced avocado (for serving)
- Sour cream (for serving)
- Lime wedges (for serving)

Instructions:

1. Preheat your oven to 375°F (190°C).
2. In a large skillet, heat the olive oil over medium heat.
3. Add the diced onion and sauté for about 3 minutes until it starts to soften.
4. Add the minced garlic and cook for another minute until fragrant.
5. Stir in the diced bell pepper, black beans, and corn. Cook for about 5-7 minutes until the vegetables are tender.
6. Season the mixture with cumin, chili powder, smoked paprika, salt, and pepper. Stir well to combine and cook for another 2 minutes.
7. Spread a thin layer of enchilada sauce over the bottom of a 9x13-inch baking dish.
8. Place about 1/3 cup of the black bean mixture in the center of each tortilla. Sprinkle some shredded cheese over the filling.
9. Roll up each tortilla tightly and place it seam-side down in the baking dish.
10. Pour the remaining enchilada sauce over the rolled tortillas, spreading it evenly.
11. Sprinkle the remaining shredded cheese over the top.
12. Cover the baking dish with aluminum foil and bake for 20 minutes.

13. Remove the foil and bake for an additional 10 minutes, or until the cheese is melted and bubbly.
14. Remove from the oven and let cool slightly.
15. Garnish with fresh cilantro, sliced avocado, and a dollop of sour cream.
16. Serve with lime wedges and enjoy your delicious black bean enchiladas!

Veggie Fajitas

Ingredients:

- 2 tablespoons olive oil
- 1 red bell pepper, sliced
- 1 yellow bell pepper, sliced
- 1 green bell pepper, sliced
- 1 large onion, sliced
- 1 zucchini, sliced into thin strips
- 1 cup mushrooms, sliced
- 1 teaspoon ground cumin
- 1 teaspoon chili powder
- 1/2 teaspoon smoked paprika
- 1/2 teaspoon garlic powder
- Salt and pepper to taste
- 8 small flour or corn tortillas
- Fresh cilantro, chopped (for garnish)
- Lime wedges
- Sliced avocado (for serving)
- Salsa (for serving)
- Sour cream (optional)
- Shredded cheese (optional)

Instructions:

1. In a large skillet, heat the olive oil over medium-high heat.
2. Add the sliced bell peppers, onion, zucchini, and mushrooms to the skillet. Sauté for about 8-10 minutes until the vegetables are tender and slightly charred.
3. Season the vegetables with ground cumin, chili powder, smoked paprika, garlic powder, salt, and pepper. Stir well to coat the vegetables evenly with the spices and cook for another 2-3 minutes.
4. Warm the tortillas in a dry skillet or microwave.
5. To assemble the fajitas, place a generous amount of the sautéed vegetables onto each tortilla.
6. Garnish with fresh cilantro and a squeeze of lime juice.
7. If desired, add sliced avocado, salsa, sour cream, and shredded cheese.
8. Serve immediately and enjoy your delicious veggie fajitas!

Chiles Rellenos

Ingredients:

- 6 large poblano peppers
- 1 cup shredded cheese (cheddar, Monterey Jack, or a blend)
- 1/2 cup all-purpose flour
- 4 large eggs, separated
- 1/4 teaspoon salt
- 1/4 teaspoon baking powder
- Vegetable oil, for frying
- 2 cups enchilada sauce (store-bought or homemade)

Instructions:

1. **Roast the Poblano Peppers:**
    1. Preheat the broiler. Place the poblano peppers on a baking sheet and broil, turning occasionally, until the skins are blackened and blistered (about 5-7 minutes per side).
    2. Transfer the peppers to a bowl and cover with plastic wrap or a towel. Let them steam for about 10 minutes to loosen the skins.
    3. Peel off the charred skins, being careful not to tear the peppers. Make a small slit down the side of each pepper and remove the seeds.
2. **Prepare the Cheese Filling:**
    1. Stuff each roasted poblano pepper with about 2-3 tablespoons of shredded cheese, then gently press the pepper closed around the filling.
3. **Prepare the Batter:**
    1. In a medium bowl, whisk the egg whites until stiff peaks form.
    2. In a separate bowl, whisk the egg yolks, salt, and baking powder until well combined.
    3. Gently fold the egg yolk mixture into the egg whites until fully incorporated.
4. **Coat and Fry the Peppers:**
    1. Heat about 1/2 inch of vegetable oil in a large skillet over medium-high heat.
    2. Lightly coat each stuffed pepper with flour, then dip into the egg batter, ensuring they are fully coated.
    3. Carefully place the coated peppers in the hot oil and fry until golden brown on all sides, about 2-3 minutes per side. Use a slotted spoon to transfer the fried peppers to a paper towel-lined plate to drain excess oil.

5. **Serve:**
    1. Warm the enchilada sauce in a small saucepan over low heat.
    2. Serve the Chiles Rellenos with a generous drizzle of enchilada sauce on top.
    3. Garnish with additional shredded cheese, fresh cilantro, and a lime wedge if desired.

Enjoy your delicious Chiles Rellenos!

Spinach and Mushroom Quesadillas

Ingredients:

- 1 tablespoon olive oil
- 1 small onion, finely chopped
- 2 cloves garlic, minced
- 1 cup mushrooms, sliced
- 4 cups fresh spinach, roughly chopped
- Salt and pepper to taste
- 1 teaspoon ground cumin
- 1/2 teaspoon chili powder
- 4 large flour tortillas
- 2 cups shredded cheese (cheddar, Monterey Jack, or a blend)
- Sour cream (for serving)
- Salsa (for serving)
- Fresh cilantro, chopped (for garnish)

Instructions:

1. **Prepare the Filling:**
    1. Heat the olive oil in a large skillet over medium heat.
    2. Add the chopped onion and sauté for about 3 minutes until it starts to soften.
    3. Add the minced garlic and cook for another minute until fragrant.
    4. Add the sliced mushrooms to the skillet and cook for about 5-7 minutes until they release their moisture and begin to brown.
    5. Stir in the chopped spinach and cook until wilted, about 2-3 minutes.
    6. Season the mixture with salt, pepper, ground cumin, and chili powder. Stir well to combine and cook for another minute.
    7. Remove the skillet from heat and set aside.
2. **Assemble the Quesadillas:**
    1. Place one tortilla on a flat surface and spread about 1/2 cup of shredded cheese over half of the tortilla.
    2. Spoon a quarter of the spinach and mushroom mixture over the cheese.
    3. Sprinkle another 1/4 cup of shredded cheese on top of the vegetable mixture.
    4. Fold the tortilla in half to enclose the filling.
    5. Repeat with the remaining tortillas and filling.
3. **Cook the Quesadillas:**

1. Heat a large skillet or griddle over medium heat.
2. Place one assembled quesadilla in the skillet and cook for 2-3 minutes on each side, or until the tortilla is golden brown and the cheese is melted.
3. Remove the cooked quesadilla from the skillet and repeat with the remaining quesadillas.
4. **Serve:**
    1. Cut each quesadilla into wedges and serve with sour cream, salsa, and fresh cilantro.

Enjoy your delicious Spinach and Mushroom Quesadillas!

Mexican Street Corn (Elote)

Ingredients:

- 6 ears of corn, husked
- 1/2 cup mayonnaise
- 1/2 cup sour cream or Mexican crema
- 1/2 cup finely grated cotija cheese (or substitute feta cheese)
- 1 teaspoon chili powder (adjust to taste)
- 1/2 teaspoon smoked paprika (optional)
- 1/4 cup chopped fresh cilantro (optional)
- Lime wedges, for serving
- Salt and pepper, to taste

Instructions:

1. **Grill the Corn:**
   - Preheat your grill to medium-high heat.
   - Place the husked ears of corn directly on the grill grates. Grill, turning occasionally, until the corn is tender and lightly charred in spots, about 10-12 minutes.
2. **Prepare the Elote Sauce:**
   - In a small bowl, mix together the mayonnaise, sour cream or Mexican crema, and half of the grated cotija cheese. Add chili powder and smoked paprika (if using), and mix until well combined. Season with salt and pepper to taste.
3. **Assemble the Elote:**
   - Once the corn is grilled, brush each ear with the prepared sauce, ensuring it coats the corn evenly.
   - Sprinkle the remaining grated cotija cheese generously over each ear of corn.
   - Optionally, sprinkle chopped cilantro over the corn for added freshness and flavor.
4. **Serve:**
   - Serve the Mexican Street Corn hot, with lime wedges on the side for squeezing over the corn.
   - Enjoy immediately as a delicious side dish or snack!

Notes:

- If you don't have a grill, you can boil or steam the corn instead. After cooking, you can char the corn in a hot skillet for a similar effect.
- Adjust the spiciness by adding more or less chili powder according to your preference.
- Cotija cheese is traditional, but if you can't find it, crumbled feta cheese makes a good substitute.

Mexican Street Corn (Elote) is a delightful treat that captures the flavors of Mexican cuisine with its creamy, cheesy, and slightly spicy coating. Enjoy it as part of your next Mexican-inspired meal!

Mexican Street Corn (Elote)

Ingredients:

- 6 ears of corn, husked
- 1/2 cup mayonnaise
- 1/2 cup sour cream or Mexican crema
- 1/2 cup finely grated cotija cheese (or substitute feta cheese)
- 1 teaspoon chili powder (adjust to taste)
- 1/2 teaspoon smoked paprika (optional)
- 1/4 cup chopped fresh cilantro (optional)
- Lime wedges, for serving
- Salt and pepper, to taste

Instructions:

1. **Grill the Corn:**
   - Preheat your grill to medium-high heat.
   - Place the husked ears of corn directly on the grill grates. Grill, turning occasionally, until the corn is tender and lightly charred in spots, about 10-12 minutes.
2. **Prepare the Elote Sauce:**
   - In a small bowl, mix together the mayonnaise, sour cream or Mexican crema, and half of the grated cotija cheese. Add chili powder and smoked paprika (if using), and mix until well combined. Season with salt and pepper to taste.
3. **Assemble the Elote:**
   - Once the corn is grilled, brush each ear with the prepared sauce, ensuring it coats the corn evenly.
   - Sprinkle the remaining grated cotija cheese generously over each ear of corn.
   - Optionally, sprinkle chopped cilantro over the corn for added freshness and flavor.
4. **Serve:**
   - Serve the Mexican Street Corn hot, with lime wedges on the side for squeezing over the corn.
   - Enjoy immediately as a delicious side dish or snack!

Notes:

- If you don't have a grill, you can boil or steam the corn instead. After cooking, you can char the corn in a hot skillet for a similar effect.
- Adjust the spiciness by adding more or less chili powder according to your preference.
- Cotija cheese is traditional, but if you can't find it, crumbled feta cheese makes a good substitute.

Mexican Street Corn (Elote) is a delightful treat that captures the flavors of Mexican cuisine with its creamy, cheesy, and slightly spicy coating. Enjoy it as part of your next Mexican-inspired meal!

Vegetarian Tamales

Ingredients:

For the Filling:

- 2 cups cooked black beans, drained and rinsed
- 1 cup corn kernels (fresh or frozen)
- 1 medium red bell pepper, diced
- 1 small onion, finely chopped
- 2 cloves garlic, minced
- 1 tablespoon olive oil
- 1 teaspoon ground cumin
- 1 teaspoon chili powder
- Salt and pepper to taste
- Fresh cilantro, chopped (optional)

For the Dough (Masa):

- 3 cups masa harina (corn flour for tamales)
- 1 1/2 cups vegetable broth or water
- 1 cup unsalted butter or vegetable shortening, softened
- 1 teaspoon baking powder
- 1 teaspoon salt

For Assembly:

- Dried corn husks, soaked in warm water for at least 30 minutes and drained
- Extra vegetable broth or water, as needed

Instructions:

1. **Prepare the Filling:**
   - Heat olive oil in a large skillet over medium heat.
   - Add chopped onion and cook until translucent, about 3-4 minutes.
   - Add minced garlic, diced bell pepper, ground cumin, chili powder, salt, and pepper. Cook for another 2-3 minutes until the bell pepper is tender.
   - Stir in black beans and corn kernels. Cook for an additional 5 minutes. Remove from heat and let the filling cool. Stir in chopped cilantro if using.
2. **Prepare the Masa Dough:**

- In a large mixing bowl, beat the softened butter or vegetable shortening with an electric mixer until fluffy.
- In a separate bowl, combine masa harina, baking powder, and salt.
- Gradually add vegetable broth or water to the butter/shortening mixture, alternating with the masa harina mixture, until a smooth dough forms. The dough should be spreadable and hold its shape.

3. **Assemble the Tamales:**
    - Spread a thin layer of masa dough onto a soaked corn husk (about 1/4 inch thick), leaving a border around the edges.
    - Place a spoonful of the filling in the center of the masa dough.
    - Fold one side of the corn husk over the filling, then fold the other side to enclose it. Fold up the narrow end of the corn husk to secure.
    - Repeat with the remaining corn husks, masa dough, and filling until all tamales are assembled.

4. **Steam the Tamales:**
    - Arrange the tamales upright in a steamer basket, open side up, with the folded end at the bottom.
    - Add water or vegetable broth to the bottom of the steamer pot, making sure it doesn't touch the tamales.
    - Cover the tamales with a layer of extra corn husks or a damp cloth, then cover tightly with a lid.
    - Steam the tamales over medium heat for 60-90 minutes, or until the masa dough is firm and pulls away easily from the corn husks.

5. **Serve:**
    - Let the tamales cool slightly before unwrapping and serving.
    - Serve with salsa, guacamole, or your favorite toppings.

Enjoy your homemade vegetarian tamales, a delicious and traditional Mexican dish that's perfect for sharing with friends and family!

Stuffed Poblano Peppers

Ingredients:

For the Peppers:

- 6 large poblano peppers
- 1 tablespoon olive oil
- Salt and pepper, to taste

For the Filling:

- 1 cup quinoa, rinsed
- 2 cups vegetable broth or water
- 1 tablespoon olive oil
- 1 small onion, finely chopped
- 2 cloves garlic, minced
- 1 can black beans, drained and rinsed
- 1 cup corn kernels (fresh or frozen)
- 1 teaspoon ground cumin
- 1 teaspoon chili powder
- Salt and pepper, to taste
- 1 cup shredded cheese (cheddar, Monterey Jack, or a blend), divided
- Fresh cilantro, chopped (optional)

For Serving:

- Salsa
- Sour cream or Greek yogurt
- Avocado slices
- Lime wedges

Instructions:

1. **Prepare the Poblano Peppers:**
    - Preheat the oven to 400°F (200°C).
    - Place the whole poblano peppers on a baking sheet lined with parchment paper.
    - Drizzle with olive oil and season with salt and pepper.

- Roast in the oven for about 20-25 minutes, turning halfway through, until the peppers are tender and lightly charred. Remove from the oven and let cool slightly.

2. **Prepare the Quinoa:**
   - In a medium saucepan, bring the vegetable broth or water to a boil.
   - Add the rinsed quinoa, reduce heat to low, cover, and simmer for 15-20 minutes, or until quinoa is cooked and liquid is absorbed. Remove from heat and fluff with a fork.

3. **Prepare the Filling:**
   - In a large skillet, heat olive oil over medium heat.
   - Add chopped onion and cook until translucent, about 3-4 minutes.
   - Add minced garlic, ground cumin, and chili powder. Cook for another minute until fragrant.
   - Stir in black beans and corn kernels. Cook for 3-4 minutes until heated through.
   - Add cooked quinoa to the skillet and stir to combine.
   - Season with salt and pepper to taste. Remove from heat and let cool slightly.
   - Stir in 1/2 cup shredded cheese and chopped cilantro if using.

4. **Assemble and Bake:**
   - Carefully make a slit along one side of each roasted poblano pepper, creating a pocket for the filling. Remove seeds and membranes if desired.
   - Spoon the quinoa and bean filling into each poblano pepper, dividing evenly among them.
   - Place the stuffed peppers back on the baking sheet. Sprinkle the remaining 1/2 cup shredded cheese over the tops of the peppers.
   - Bake in the oven at 400°F (200°C) for 15-20 minutes, or until the cheese is melted and bubbly.

5. **Serve:**
   - Remove from the oven and let cool slightly before serving.
   - Serve stuffed poblano peppers with salsa, sour cream or Greek yogurt, avocado slices, and lime wedges on the side.

Enjoy your flavorful and satisfying Stuffed Poblano Peppers!

Sweet Potato and Black Bean Burritos

Ingredients:

For the Sweet Potatoes:

- 2 medium sweet potatoes, peeled and diced into small cubes
- 1 tablespoon olive oil
- 1 teaspoon ground cumin
- 1/2 teaspoon chili powder
- Salt and pepper, to taste

For the Black Beans:

- 1 tablespoon olive oil
- 1 small onion, finely chopped
- 2 cloves garlic, minced
- 1 can black beans, drained and rinsed
- 1 teaspoon ground cumin
- 1/2 teaspoon chili powder
- Salt and pepper, to taste
- 1/4 cup water or vegetable broth

For Assembly:

- 4 large flour tortillas
- 1 cup shredded cheese (cheddar, Monterey Jack, or a blend)
- Fresh cilantro, chopped (optional)
- Salsa, guacamole, or sour cream (for serving)

Instructions:

1. **Prepare the Sweet Potatoes:**
   - Preheat the oven to 400°F (200°C).
   - Toss the diced sweet potatoes with olive oil, ground cumin, chili powder, salt, and pepper on a baking sheet.
   - Roast in the oven for 20-25 minutes, or until tender and lightly browned, stirring halfway through. Remove from the oven and set aside.
2. **Prepare the Black Beans:**
   - Heat olive oil in a large skillet over medium heat.
   - Add chopped onion and cook until translucent, about 3-4 minutes.

- Add minced garlic, ground cumin, and chili powder. Cook for another minute until fragrant.
- Stir in black beans and water or vegetable broth. Cook for 5-7 minutes, stirring occasionally, until heated through and slightly thickened. Season with salt and pepper to taste. Remove from heat.

3. **Assemble the Burritos:**
   - Warm the flour tortillas in a dry skillet or microwave until soft and pliable.
   - Spoon a portion of the roasted sweet potatoes and black bean mixture onto each tortilla, dividing evenly.
   - Sprinkle shredded cheese over the filling, and add chopped cilantro if desired.

4. **Roll the Burritos:**
   - Fold in the sides of each tortilla, then roll up tightly from the bottom to enclose the filling.

5. **Serve:**
   - Place the assembled burritos seam-side down on a serving plate.
   - Serve with salsa, guacamole, or sour cream on the side.

Enjoy your flavorful Sweet Potato and Black Bean Burritos, perfect for a satisfying vegetarian meal!

Mexican Rice

Ingredients:

- 1 cup long-grain white rice
- 1 tablespoon vegetable oil or olive oil
- 1/2 onion, finely chopped
- 2 cloves garlic, minced
- 1 can (14.5 oz) diced tomatoes, undrained
- 1 3/4 cups vegetable broth or chicken broth
- 1 teaspoon ground cumin
- 1 teaspoon chili powder (adjust to taste for spiciness)
- Salt and pepper, to taste
- Fresh cilantro, chopped (optional, for garnish)
- Lime wedges (for serving)

Instructions:

1. **Rinse and Toast the Rice:**
   - Rinse the rice under cold water until the water runs clear. This helps remove excess starch and prevents the rice from becoming sticky.
   - Heat the vegetable oil in a large skillet or saucepan over medium heat. Add the rinsed rice and toast it, stirring frequently, until it turns golden brown, about 5-7 minutes.
2. **Prepare the Aromatics:**
   - Add the chopped onion to the skillet with the toasted rice. Cook for 2-3 minutes until the onion starts to soften.
   - Stir in the minced garlic and cook for another minute until fragrant.
3. **Simmer with Tomatoes and Broth:**
   - Add the diced tomatoes (including their juices) to the skillet with the rice and onions. Stir to combine.
   - Pour in the vegetable broth or chicken broth, and add ground cumin, chili powder, salt, and pepper. Stir well to combine.
4. **Cook the Rice:**
   - Bring the mixture to a boil, then reduce the heat to low. Cover the skillet with a lid and simmer for 20-25 minutes, or until the rice is tender and the liquid is absorbed.
5. **Fluff and Serve:**
   - Once the rice is cooked, remove the skillet from heat and let it sit covered for 5 minutes.

- Fluff the rice with a fork to separate the grains. Taste and adjust seasoning if needed.
- Garnish with chopped cilantro if desired, and serve with lime wedges on the side for squeezing over the rice.

Enjoy your flavorful and aromatic Mexican Rice (Arroz Rojo) as a perfect complement to your favorite Mexican dishes!

Guacamole

Ingredients:

- 3 ripe avocados
- 1 lime, juiced
- 1/2 teaspoon salt, or more to taste
- 1/2 teaspoon ground cumin (optional)
- 1/2 teaspoon cayenne pepper or paprika (optional, for spiciness)
- 1/2 cup red onion, finely diced
- 1/2 cup tomato, diced and seeds removed (optional)
- 2 tablespoons fresh cilantro, chopped
- 1-2 cloves garlic, minced (optional)
- Jalapeño or serrano pepper, finely diced (optional, for heat)

Instructions:

1. **Prepare the Avocados:**
    - Cut the avocados in half and remove the pits. Scoop out the flesh into a mixing bowl.
2. **Mash the Avocados:**
    - Using a fork or potato masher, mash the avocado until it reaches your desired consistency (smooth or chunky).
3. **Season the Guacamole:**
    - Add lime juice, salt, ground cumin, and cayenne pepper or paprika (if using). Mix well to combine.
4. **Add Additional Ingredients:**
    - Stir in diced red onion, diced tomato (if using), chopped cilantro, minced garlic (if using), and diced jalapeño or serrano pepper (if using). Mix gently to incorporate all ingredients evenly.
5. **Taste and Adjust:**
    - Taste the guacamole and adjust seasoning as needed, adding more salt or lime juice to balance the flavors.
6. **Serve:**
    - Transfer the guacamole to a serving bowl. For best flavor, cover the guacamole with plastic wrap directly on its surface to prevent browning, and refrigerate until ready to serve.
    - Serve with tortilla chips, as a topping for tacos, burritos, or any Mexican-inspired dish.

Tips:

- To keep guacamole from browning, store it in an airtight container with plastic wrap pressed directly onto the surface of the guacamole to limit exposure to air.
- Adjust the spiciness to your preference by adding more or less jalapeño or serrano pepper.
- For a smoother guacamole, use a blender or food processor instead of mashing by hand.

Enjoy your homemade guacamole as a flavorful and creamy dip or topping!

Vegetarian Tortilla Soup

Ingredients:

- 2 tablespoons olive oil
- 1 medium onion, chopped
- 2 cloves garlic, minced
- 1 jalapeño, seeded and minced (optional, for heat)
- 1 red bell pepper, chopped
- 1 zucchini, diced
- 1 cup corn kernels (fresh or frozen)
- 1 can (14 oz) diced tomatoes
- 4 cups vegetable broth
- 1 teaspoon ground cumin
- 1 teaspoon chili powder
- 1/2 teaspoon smoked paprika
- Salt and pepper, to taste
- 1 can (15 oz) black beans, drained and rinsed
- Juice of 1 lime
- Fresh cilantro, chopped, for garnish
- Tortilla chips, crushed, for serving
- Avocado slices, for serving
- Sour cream or Greek yogurt, for serving
- Lime wedges, for serving

Instructions:

1. **Sauté Aromatics:**
   - Heat olive oil in a large pot or Dutch oven over medium heat. Add chopped onion and cook until translucent, about 5 minutes.
   - Add minced garlic and jalapeño (if using), and cook for another minute until fragrant.
2. **Add Vegetables and Spices:**
   - Stir in chopped red bell pepper, diced zucchini, and corn kernels. Cook for about 5 minutes until vegetables start to soften.
   - Add diced tomatoes with their juices, vegetable broth, ground cumin, chili powder, smoked paprika, salt, and pepper. Stir well to combine.
3. **Simmer the Soup:**
   - Bring the soup to a boil, then reduce heat to low and let it simmer uncovered for 15-20 minutes, stirring occasionally.

4. **Add Black Beans and Lime Juice:**
   - Stir in drained and rinsed black beans. Simmer for another 5 minutes until heated through.
   - Add lime juice to the soup and stir to incorporate.
5. **Serve:**
   - Ladle the vegetarian tortilla soup into bowls.
   - Top each bowl with crushed tortilla chips, avocado slices, a dollop of sour cream or Greek yogurt, and chopped fresh cilantro.
   - Serve with lime wedges on the side for squeezing over the soup.

Optional Additions:

- For added protein, you can stir in cooked quinoa, shredded chicken (if not strictly vegetarian), or tofu cubes.
- Adjust the spiciness by adding more jalapeño or chili powder according to your taste preference.
- For a creamier soup, stir in a bit of coconut milk or cashew cream before serving.

Enjoy your hearty and flavorful Vegetarian Tortilla Soup!

Roasted Vegetable Tostadas

Ingredients:

For the Roasted Vegetables:

- 2 bell peppers (any color), seeded and sliced
- 1 large red onion, sliced
- 1 zucchini, sliced into rounds
- 1 small eggplant, diced
- 2 tablespoons olive oil
- 1 teaspoon ground cumin
- 1 teaspoon chili powder
- Salt and pepper, to taste

For the Tostadas:

- 8 small corn or flour tortillas
- Olive oil spray or cooking spray
- 1 can (15 oz) black beans, drained and rinsed
- 1 cup shredded cheese (cheddar, Monterey Jack, or a blend)
- Fresh cilantro, chopped, for garnish
- Lime wedges, for serving

Optional Toppings:

- Salsa
- Guacamole or sliced avocado
- Sour cream or Greek yogurt
- Pickled jalapeños

Instructions:

1. **Roast the Vegetables:**
   - Preheat the oven to 400°F (200°C).
   - Place sliced bell peppers, red onion, zucchini rounds, and diced eggplant on a large baking sheet.
   - Drizzle with olive oil and sprinkle with ground cumin, chili powder, salt, and pepper. Toss to coat evenly.
   - Roast in the preheated oven for 20-25 minutes, stirring halfway through, until the vegetables are tender and slightly caramelized.

2. **Prepare the Tostadas:**
    - While the vegetables are roasting, arrange the tortillas in a single layer on another baking sheet.
    - Lightly spray both sides of each tortilla with olive oil spray or cooking spray.
    - Bake in the oven at 400°F (200°C) for 8-10 minutes, flipping halfway through, until the tortillas are golden and crispy.
3. **Assemble the Tostadas:**
    - Spread a layer of black beans on each crispy tortilla.
    - Top with a generous amount of roasted vegetables.
    - Sprinkle shredded cheese over the vegetables while they are still warm, allowing it to melt slightly.
    - Garnish with chopped fresh cilantro and serve with lime wedges on the side.
4. **Serve:**
    - Serve the roasted vegetable tostadas immediately, offering optional toppings such as salsa, guacamole or avocado slices, sour cream or Greek yogurt, and pickled jalapeños on the side.
    - Enjoy your flavorful and colorful roasted vegetable tostadas!

This dish is not only delicious but also versatile, allowing you to customize the toppings according to your preferences. It's perfect for a hearty and satisfying vegetarian meal!

Cheese and Bean Pupusas

Ingredients:

For the Pupusa Dough:

- 2 cups masa harina (corn flour for pupusas)
- 1 1/4 cups warm water
- 1/2 teaspoon salt

For the Filling:

- 1 cup refried beans (homemade or canned)
- 1 cup shredded cheese (queso fresco, mozzarella, or your choice)

For Serving:

- Curtido (Salvadoran cabbage slaw, optional)
- Salsa roja or salsa verde
- Sour cream or crema

Instructions:

1. **Prepare the Pupusa Dough:**
   - In a large bowl, mix masa harina and salt together.
   - Gradually add warm water and knead until a smooth dough forms. The dough should be soft and pliable, similar to Play-Doh consistency. If it's too dry, add a little more water; if too wet, add more masa harina.
   - Divide the dough into 8 equal portions and roll each portion into a ball.
2. **Prepare the Filling:**
   - In a small bowl, mix together refried beans and shredded cheese until well combined.
3. **Assemble the Pupusas:**
   - Take one dough ball and use your thumb to make an indentation in the center. Gradually press and flatten the dough ball into a circle about 4-5 inches in diameter, making sure the edges are slightly thicker than the center.
   - Spoon about 2 tablespoons of the bean and cheese filling into the center of the dough circle.

- Gently fold the edges of the dough over the filling, pinching them together to seal. Flatten the filled dough ball into a disc about 1/4 to 1/2 inch thick, ensuring the filling is evenly distributed and sealed inside.

4. **Cook the Pupusas:**
    - Heat a lightly oiled skillet or griddle over medium-high heat.
    - Carefully place each pupusa on the hot skillet and cook for about 3-4 minutes on each side, or until golden brown and slightly crisp. Press down gently with a spatula during cooking to ensure even cooking and to flatten the pupusa slightly.
    - Repeat with the remaining dough balls and filling.
5. **Serve:**
    - Serve the cheese and bean pupusas warm with curtido (cabbage slaw), salsa roja or salsa verde, and sour cream or crema on the side.
    - Enjoy your delicious and authentic Cheese and Bean Pupusas!

Notes:

- Curtido (Salvadoran cabbage slaw) is a traditional accompaniment to pupusas and adds a delicious crunch and tanginess. You can find recipes online to make curtido at home.
- Pupusas are best enjoyed fresh and hot off the griddle. If preparing ahead, you can store cooked pupusas in a warm oven until ready to serve.

These pupusas are a delightful combination of cheesy, savory filling encased in a crispy corn dough, perfect for a satisfying meal or snack!

Avocado Salad

Ingredients:

- 2 ripe avocados, diced
- 1 pint cherry tomatoes, halved
- 1/2 red onion, thinly sliced
- 1 cucumber, diced
- 1/4 cup fresh cilantro, chopped
- Juice of 1-2 limes, to taste
- 2 tablespoons extra virgin olive oil
- Salt and pepper, to taste
- Optional: crumbled feta cheese, sliced jalapeños, or chopped fresh parsley for garnish

Instructions:

1. **Prepare the Ingredients:**
   - Dice the avocados and place them in a large salad bowl.
   - Halve the cherry tomatoes, thinly slice the red onion, dice the cucumber, and chop the fresh cilantro. Add them to the bowl with the avocados.
2. **Make the Dressing:**
   - In a small bowl, whisk together the lime juice, extra virgin olive oil, salt, and pepper until well combined. Adjust the seasoning to taste.
3. **Assemble the Salad:**
   - Drizzle the dressing over the avocado and vegetable mixture in the salad bowl.
   - Gently toss the salad ingredients together until everything is evenly coated with the dressing.
4. **Serve:**
   - Transfer the avocado salad to a serving dish or individual salad plates.
   - If desired, sprinkle crumbled feta cheese, sliced jalapeños, or chopped fresh parsley on top for extra flavor and garnish.
5. **Enjoy:**
   - Serve the avocado salad immediately as a refreshing side dish or light meal.
   - This salad pairs well with grilled chicken, fish, or as a topping for tacos or quesadillas.

Tips:

- To prevent the avocados from browning, assemble the salad just before serving and coat them well with lime juice.
- Customize the salad by adding other ingredients such as black beans, corn kernels, or bell peppers for additional flavor and texture.

This Avocado Salad is not only delicious but also packed with healthy fats, vitamins, and antioxidants, making it a perfect addition to any meal or as a standalone dish.

Mexican Stuffed Peppers

Ingredients:

- 4 large bell peppers (any color), tops cut off and seeds removed
- 1 tablespoon olive oil
- 1 small onion, diced
- 2 cloves garlic, minced
- 1 jalapeño, seeded and diced (optional, for heat)
- 1 teaspoon ground cumin
- 1 teaspoon chili powder
- 1/2 teaspoon smoked paprika
- Salt and pepper, to taste
- 1 cup cooked quinoa or rice
- 1 can (15 oz) black beans, drained and rinsed
- 1 cup corn kernels (fresh or frozen)
- 1 cup diced tomatoes
- 1 cup shredded cheese (cheddar, Monterey Jack, or a blend), divided
- Fresh cilantro, chopped, for garnish
- Lime wedges, for serving

Instructions:

1. **Prepare the Bell Peppers:**
    - Preheat the oven to 375°F (190°C).
    - Cut the tops off the bell peppers and remove the seeds and membranes. Place them upright in a baking dish.
2. **Prepare the Filling:**
    - In a large skillet, heat olive oil over medium heat.
    - Add diced onion and cook until translucent, about 5 minutes.
    - Add minced garlic and jalapeño (if using), and cook for another minute until fragrant.
    - Stir in ground cumin, chili powder, smoked paprika, salt, and pepper.
    - Add cooked quinoa or rice, black beans, corn kernels, and diced tomatoes to the skillet. Stir well to combine and cook for 5-7 minutes until heated through.
    - Stir in half of the shredded cheese until melted and well combined.
3. **Stuff the Peppers:**
    - Spoon the filling mixture evenly into each prepared bell pepper, pressing gently to pack the filling.

- Sprinkle the remaining shredded cheese over the tops of the stuffed peppers.

4. **Bake the Stuffed Peppers:**
    - Cover the baking dish with foil and bake in the preheated oven for 30-35 minutes, or until the peppers are tender and the filling is heated through.
    - Remove the foil during the last 10 minutes of baking to allow the cheese to melt and slightly brown.

5. **Serve:**
    - Remove the stuffed peppers from the oven and let them cool slightly.
    - Garnish with chopped fresh cilantro and serve with lime wedges on the side for squeezing over the peppers.
    - Enjoy your delicious and hearty Mexican Stuffed Peppers!

Tips:

- Customize the filling by adding diced avocado, chopped spinach, or your favorite vegetables.
- For a spicier version, leave the seeds in the jalapeño or add a dash of hot sauce to the filling mixture.
- These stuffed peppers can be made ahead of time and stored in the refrigerator. Reheat them in the oven or microwave before serving.

This recipe provides a satisfying and flavorful meal that's packed with Mexican-inspired ingredients and perfect for a family dinner or gathering with friends.

Veggie Nachos

Ingredients:

- 1 bag (about 10 oz) tortilla chips
- 1 can (15 oz) black beans, drained and rinsed
- 1 cup corn kernels (fresh or frozen)
- 1 cup cherry tomatoes, halved
- 1/2 red onion, finely diced
- 1 bell pepper (any color), diced
- 1 jalapeño, thinly sliced (optional, for heat)
- 1 cup shredded cheese (cheddar, Monterey Jack, or a blend)
- 1 avocado, diced
- Fresh cilantro, chopped, for garnish
- Lime wedges, for serving
- Salsa, guacamole, sour cream, or Greek yogurt, for serving

Instructions:

1. **Preheat the Oven:**
   - Preheat your oven to 400°F (200°C).
2. **Prepare the Nachos:**
   - Spread the tortilla chips in a single layer on a large baking sheet or oven-safe dish.
3. **Assemble the Nachos:**
   - Sprinkle black beans, corn kernels, cherry tomatoes, red onion, bell pepper, and jalapeño slices (if using) evenly over the tortilla chips.
   - Sprinkle shredded cheese over the top of the nachos, covering all the ingredients.
4. **Bake the Nachos:**
   - Place the baking sheet or dish in the preheated oven and bake for about 10-15 minutes, or until the cheese is melted and bubbly.
5. **Add Toppings:**
   - Remove the nachos from the oven and immediately top with diced avocado and chopped cilantro.
   - Serve hot with lime wedges on the side for squeezing over the nachos.
6. **Serve:**
   - Serve the veggie nachos immediately with salsa, guacamole, sour cream, or Greek yogurt on the side for dipping or drizzling.

Tips:

- Customize your veggie nachos by adding other toppings such as black olives, diced jalapeños, sliced scallions, or even a drizzle of hot sauce.
- For a creamier texture, you can layer some refried beans or spread a thin layer of guacamole on the tortilla chips before adding the toppings.
- Make sure to distribute the toppings evenly to ensure each nacho chip is loaded with flavor.

Veggie Nachos make a perfect appetizer for parties or a satisfying meal for a casual dinner. They are versatile, colorful, and packed with delicious flavors that everyone will enjoy!

Cilantro Lime Rice

Ingredients:

- 1 cup long-grain white rice
- 1 3/4 cups water or vegetable broth
- 1 tablespoon olive oil or butter
- 1 clove garlic, minced (optional)
- Juice of 1-2 limes, to taste
- Zest of 1 lime (optional, for extra lime flavor)
- 1/4 cup fresh cilantro, chopped
- Salt, to taste

Instructions:

1. **Rinse the Rice:**
   - Rinse the rice under cold water until the water runs clear. This helps remove excess starch for fluffy rice.
2. **Cook the Rice:**
   - In a medium saucepan, heat olive oil or butter over medium heat. Add minced garlic (if using) and sauté for about 1 minute until fragrant.
   - Add the rinsed rice to the saucepan and stir to coat with the oil or butter. Cook for 1-2 minutes, stirring occasionally, until the rice starts to toast slightly.
   - Pour in water or vegetable broth and bring to a boil.
   - Reduce heat to low, cover the saucepan with a lid, and simmer for 15-20 minutes, or until the rice is tender and the liquid is absorbed.
3. **Fluff the Rice:**
   - Once the rice is cooked, remove the saucepan from heat and let it sit covered for 5 minutes.
   - Remove the lid and fluff the rice with a fork to separate the grains.
4. **Add Cilantro and Lime:**
   - Add freshly squeezed lime juice (start with juice of 1 lime) and chopped cilantro to the rice. Add lime zest if using for extra flavor.
   - Season with salt to taste and gently toss to combine all ingredients evenly.
5. **Serve:**
   - Transfer the cilantro lime rice to a serving dish and garnish with additional chopped cilantro if desired.
   - Serve hot as a side dish with your favorite Mexican or Tex-Mex meals.

Tips:

- For a richer flavor, cook the rice in vegetable broth instead of water.
- Adjust the amount of lime juice according to your preference for tanginess.
- If you prefer a milder garlic flavor, you can omit the minced garlic or reduce the amount.

Cilantro Lime Rice adds a zesty and aromatic twist to plain rice, making it a perfect accompaniment to dishes like burritos, tacos, enchiladas, or grilled meats. Enjoy its vibrant flavors!

Refried Beans

Ingredients:

- 2 cups cooked pinto beans (or 2 cans, drained and rinsed)
- 2 tablespoons vegetable oil or olive oil
- 1/2 onion, finely chopped
- 2 cloves garlic, minced
- 1/2 teaspoon ground cumin
- 1/2 teaspoon chili powder
- Salt, to taste
- 1/2 cup vegetable broth or water (more if needed)
- Optional toppings: chopped cilantro, shredded cheese, sour cream, sliced jalapeños

Instructions:

1. **Prepare the Beans:**
    - If using canned beans, drain and rinse them thoroughly. If using cooked beans, skip this step.
2. **Sauté Aromatics:**
    - Heat vegetable oil or olive oil in a large skillet or saucepan over medium heat.
    - Add chopped onion and cook until softened and translucent, about 5 minutes.
    - Add minced garlic, ground cumin, and chili powder. Cook for another 1-2 minutes until fragrant.
3. **Mash the Beans:**
    - Add the cooked pinto beans to the skillet. Using a potato masher or the back of a spoon, mash the beans to your desired consistency. Some prefer a smoother texture, while others enjoy leaving some beans whole.
4. **Cook the Beans:**
    - Pour in vegetable broth or water gradually, stirring continuously, until the beans reach a creamy consistency. Add more liquid if needed to achieve the desired texture.
    - Season with salt to taste.
5. **Simmer and Serve:**
    - Reduce the heat to low and simmer the refried beans for 10-15 minutes, stirring occasionally, to allow the flavors to meld together.

        - Remove from heat and serve hot as a side dish, filling for tacos and burritos, or as a dip.
    6. **Optional Toppings:**
        - Garnish with chopped cilantro, shredded cheese, a dollop of sour cream, or sliced jalapeños before serving, if desired.

Tips:

- For a spicier version, add a pinch of cayenne pepper or chopped jalapeños during cooking.
- Adjust the consistency of the refried beans by adding more or less liquid according to your preference.
- Leftover refried beans can be stored in an airtight container in the refrigerator for up to 4-5 days or frozen for longer storage.

Homemade refried beans are versatile, economical, and packed with flavor, making them a perfect addition to your Mexican-inspired meals!

Vegetarian Pozole

Ingredients:

- 2 tablespoons olive oil
- 1 large onion, chopped
- 4 cloves garlic, minced
- 1 jalapeño or poblano pepper, seeded and diced (adjust to taste)
- 1 red bell pepper, chopped
- 1 zucchini, diced
- 2 carrots, diced
- 1 teaspoon ground cumin
- 1 teaspoon chili powder
- 1/2 teaspoon smoked paprika
- 1 teaspoon dried oregano
- Salt and pepper, to taste
- 1 can (15 oz) hominy, drained and rinsed
- 1 can (15 oz) diced tomatoes
- 6 cups vegetable broth
- 1 lime, juiced
- Fresh cilantro, chopped, for garnish
- Radishes, sliced, for garnish
- Avocado slices, for garnish
- Tortilla chips or strips, for serving

Instructions:

1. **Sauté Aromatics:**
   - Heat olive oil in a large pot or Dutch oven over medium heat.
   - Add chopped onion and cook until softened, about 5 minutes.
   - Stir in minced garlic, diced jalapeño or poblano pepper, and red bell pepper. Cook for another 3-4 minutes until fragrant.
2. **Add Vegetables and Spices:**
   - Add diced zucchini and carrots to the pot. Stir in ground cumin, chili powder, smoked paprika, dried oregano, salt, and pepper. Cook for 2-3 minutes to toast the spices and coat the vegetables.
3. **Simmer the Stew:**
   - Pour in vegetable broth, diced tomatoes (with their juices), and drained hominy. Stir well to combine.

- Bring the mixture to a boil, then reduce heat to low. Cover and simmer for 20-25 minutes, stirring occasionally, until the vegetables are tender and flavors have melded together.

4. **Finish and Serve:**
    - Remove the pot from heat and stir in fresh lime juice. Taste and adjust seasoning if needed.
    - Ladle the vegetarian pozole into bowls. Garnish with chopped fresh cilantro, sliced radishes, and avocado slices.
    - Serve hot with tortilla chips or strips on the side.

Tips:

- For added protein, you can stir in cooked beans such as black beans or kidney beans during the last 5 minutes of cooking.
- Adjust the spice level by adding more or less jalapeño or poblano pepper, or a pinch of cayenne pepper.
- Pozole is often served with additional garnishes such as shredded cabbage, diced onion, or a squeeze of extra lime juice for extra freshness.

This vegetarian pozole is comforting, nutritious, and perfect for a satisfying meal. Enjoy its rich flavors and textures with your favorite toppings!

Zucchini and Corn Tacos

Ingredients:

- 2 tablespoons olive oil
- 1 small onion, finely chopped
- 2 cloves garlic, minced
- 2 medium zucchini, diced
- 1 cup corn kernels (fresh or frozen)
- 1 teaspoon ground cumin
- 1/2 teaspoon chili powder
- Salt and pepper, to taste
- Juice of 1 lime
- 8 small corn or flour tortillas
- Optional toppings: chopped cilantro, crumbled queso fresco or feta cheese, salsa, sliced avocado, lime wedges

Instructions:

1. **Sauté the Vegetables:**
    - Heat olive oil in a large skillet over medium heat.
    - Add finely chopped onion and cook until softened, about 5 minutes.
    - Stir in minced garlic and cook for another minute until fragrant.
2. **Cook the Zucchini and Corn:**
    - Add diced zucchini to the skillet. Cook for 5-6 minutes, stirring occasionally, until zucchini begins to soften.
    - Add corn kernels, ground cumin, chili powder, salt, and pepper to the skillet. Stir well to combine.
    - Cook for an additional 3-4 minutes, or until the zucchini is tender and the corn is heated through.
    - Remove the skillet from heat and drizzle lime juice over the zucchini and corn mixture. Stir to incorporate.
3. **Warm the Tortillas:**
    - While the vegetables are cooking, heat the tortillas. You can warm them in a dry skillet over medium heat for about 30 seconds per side, or wrap them in foil and warm in the oven at 350°F (175°C) for 5-10 minutes.
4. **Assemble the Tacos:**
    - Spoon the zucchini and corn mixture evenly onto each warmed tortilla.
    - Top with optional toppings such as chopped cilantro, crumbled queso fresco or feta cheese, salsa, sliced avocado, and a squeeze of lime juice.

5. **Serve:**
    - Serve the zucchini and corn tacos immediately while warm.
    - Enjoy these flavorful and satisfying vegetarian tacos!

Tips:

- Customize the tacos with additional toppings like diced tomatoes, shredded lettuce, or a drizzle of sour cream or Greek yogurt.
- For added protein, you can include cooked black beans or refried beans as a filling or topping.
- Make a larger batch of the zucchini and corn mixture and use it as a filling for quesadillas, burritos, or enchiladas.

These zucchini and corn tacos are quick to prepare, packed with fresh flavors, and perfect for a light and delicious vegetarian meal. Enjoy them for a flavorful taco night!

Mexican Quinoa Salad

Ingredients:

- 1 cup quinoa, rinsed
- 2 cups water or vegetable broth
- 1 can (15 oz) black beans, drained and rinsed
- 1 cup corn kernels (fresh or frozen)
- 1 pint cherry tomatoes, halved
- 1 bell pepper (any color), diced
- 1/2 red onion, finely chopped
- 1 jalapeño, seeded and diced (optional, for heat)
- 1/4 cup fresh cilantro, chopped
- Juice of 2 limes
- 2 tablespoons olive oil
- 1 teaspoon ground cumin
- 1/2 teaspoon chili powder
- Salt and pepper, to taste
- Avocado slices, for garnish (optional)

Instructions:

1. **Cook the Quinoa:**
    - In a medium saucepan, bring water or vegetable broth to a boil.
    - Add rinsed quinoa, reduce heat to low, cover, and simmer for 15-20 minutes, or until quinoa is cooked and water is absorbed.
    - Remove from heat and let quinoa cool slightly.
2. **Prepare the Salad:**
    - In a large bowl, combine cooked quinoa, black beans, corn kernels, cherry tomatoes, diced bell pepper, finely chopped red onion, and diced jalapeño (if using).
    - Add chopped cilantro to the bowl.
3. **Make the Dressing:**
    - In a small bowl, whisk together lime juice, olive oil, ground cumin, chili powder, salt, and pepper until well combined.
4. **Combine and Toss:**
    - Pour the dressing over the quinoa and vegetable mixture in the bowl.
    - Toss gently to coat all ingredients evenly with the dressing.
5. **Chill and Serve:**

- Cover the salad and refrigerate for at least 30 minutes to allow flavors to meld together.
- Before serving, garnish with avocado slices if desired.

6. **Serve:**
    - Serve the Mexican Quinoa Salad chilled or at room temperature.
    - Enjoy as a refreshing and nutritious salad on its own or as a side dish with grilled chicken, fish, or as a filling for tacos or burritos.

Tips:

- Customize the salad by adding other ingredients such as diced avocado, black olives, or shredded lettuce.
- For added protein, you can mix in cooked and shredded chicken, tofu, or chickpeas.
- Store any leftover salad in an airtight container in the refrigerator for up to 3-4 days.

This Mexican Quinoa Salad is packed with protein, fiber, and vibrant flavors, making it a perfect option for a healthy lunch, dinner, or side dish for gatherings and potlucks. Enjoy its delicious combination of ingredients!

Cheese Enchiladas

Ingredients:

- 12 corn tortillas
- 2 cups shredded cheese (such as cheddar, Monterey Jack, or a blend)
- 1 small onion, finely chopped (optional)
- 2 cloves garlic, minced
- 2 tablespoons vegetable oil
- 2 cups enchilada sauce (store-bought or homemade, divided)
- Salt and pepper, to taste
- Optional toppings: chopped fresh cilantro, sour cream, diced avocado, sliced jalapeños

Instructions:

1. **Prepare the Enchilada Filling:**
    - In a skillet, heat vegetable oil over medium heat.
    - Add finely chopped onion (if using) and cook until softened, about 5 minutes.
    - Add minced garlic and cook for another minute until fragrant.
    - Remove from heat and set aside.
2. **Assemble the Enchiladas:**
    - Preheat the oven to 350°F (175°C).
    - Spread 1/2 cup of enchilada sauce evenly on the bottom of a 9x13-inch baking dish.
    - Warm the corn tortillas (you can do this in a microwave wrapped in a damp paper towel for about 30 seconds or in a dry skillet for a few seconds per side) to make them pliable.
    - Place a spoonful of the onion and garlic mixture (if using) in the center of each tortilla.
    - Sprinkle shredded cheese evenly over the onion mixture on each tortilla, reserving some cheese for topping.
3. **Roll the Enchiladas:**
    - Roll up each tortilla tightly and place seam-side down in the prepared baking dish.
    - Arrange the filled tortillas snugly next to each other to fit in the baking dish.
4. **Bake the Enchiladas:**

- Pour the remaining enchilada sauce over the rolled tortillas, spreading it evenly to cover.
- Sprinkle the reserved shredded cheese over the top.

5. **Bake:**
   - Cover the baking dish with foil and bake in the preheated oven for 20-25 minutes, or until the enchiladas are heated through and the cheese is melted and bubbly.

6. **Serve:**
   - Remove the foil from the baking dish and sprinkle chopped fresh cilantro over the enchiladas.
   - Serve hot, garnished with optional toppings such as sour cream, diced avocado, and sliced jalapeños.

Tips:

- For a smoother texture, you can blend the onion and garlic mixture with some of the enchilada sauce before spreading it on the tortillas.
- Adjust the heat level of the enchiladas by using mild or spicy enchilada sauce and adding sliced jalapeños or hot sauce to taste.
- Serve the cheese enchiladas with Mexican rice, refried beans, or a side salad for a complete meal.

These Cheese Enchiladas are comforting, cheesy, and full of flavor—a perfect dish for a family dinner or gathering with friends. Enjoy the rich, satisfying taste of homemade enchiladas!

Salsa Verde

Ingredients:

- 1 lb (about 450g) fresh tomatillos, husked and rinsed
- 1-2 jalapeño peppers (adjust to taste), stemmed and halved
- 1 small onion, quartered
- 2 cloves garlic, peeled
- 1/2 cup fresh cilantro leaves
- Juice of 1 lime
- Salt, to taste

Instructions:

1. **Prepare the Tomatillos:**
   - Remove the husks from the tomatillos and rinse them well under warm water to remove any sticky residue.
2. **Roast the Vegetables:**
   - Preheat your broiler or grill to high heat.
   - Place the tomatillos, jalapeño peppers, onion quarters, and garlic cloves on a baking sheet lined with aluminum foil.
3. **Broil or Grill:**
   - Broil or grill the vegetables for 5-7 minutes, turning occasionally, until they are charred and softened. The tomatillos should be tender and slightly blistered.
4. **Blend the Ingredients:**
   - Transfer the roasted tomatillos, jalapeños, onion, and garlic to a blender or food processor.
   - Add fresh cilantro leaves and lime juice.
5. **Blend Until Smooth:**
   - Pulse or blend until the salsa reaches your desired consistency—smooth but still with a bit of texture.
   - Season with salt to taste and blend briefly to incorporate.
6. **Serve or Store:**
   - Transfer the Salsa Verde to a bowl or airtight container.
   - Serve immediately as a dip with tortilla chips, or use it as a sauce for tacos, enchiladas, or other Mexican dishes.
   - Salsa Verde can be stored in the refrigerator for up to 1 week. It also freezes well for longer storage.

Tips:

- Adjust the spiciness of the salsa by adding more or fewer jalapeño peppers, or include the seeds for extra heat.
- If you prefer a smoother salsa, you can strain it through a fine mesh sieve after blending.
- For a roasted flavor variation, you can roast the tomatillos and other vegetables in a dry skillet over medium-high heat until charred.

Homemade Salsa Verde adds a bright and zesty flavor to your favorite Mexican dishes, enhancing their taste with its fresh ingredients and vibrant color. Enjoy experimenting with this versatile salsa in your kitchen!

Pico de Gallo

Ingredients:

- 4 medium tomatoes, diced
- 1/2 red onion, finely chopped
- 1 jalapeño or serrano pepper, seeded and finely diced
- 1/4 cup fresh cilantro, chopped
- Juice of 1 lime
- Salt, to taste

Instructions:

1. **Prepare the Ingredients:**
    - Dice the tomatoes into small pieces. Remove the seeds if you prefer a less watery texture.
    - Finely chop the red onion.
    - Seed and finely dice the jalapeño or serrano pepper. Adjust the amount according to your desired level of spiciness.
    - Chop the fresh cilantro leaves.
2. **Combine Ingredients:**
    - In a mixing bowl, combine the diced tomatoes, chopped red onion, diced jalapeño or serrano pepper, and chopped cilantro.
3. **Add Lime Juice and Salt:**
    - Squeeze the juice of one lime over the mixture.
    - Season with salt, starting with a small amount and adjusting to taste.
4. **Mix Well:**
    - Gently toss all the ingredients together until well combined.
5. **Chill and Serve:**
    - Cover the bowl with plastic wrap or transfer the Pico de Gallo to an airtight container.
    - Refrigerate for at least 30 minutes to allow the flavors to meld together.
6. **Serve:**
    - Serve Pico de Gallo as a topping for tacos, burritos, nachos, or grilled meats.
    - It can also be served as a dip with tortilla chips or as a side salad.

Tips:

- For extra flavor, you can add a minced clove of garlic or a dash of ground cumin to the Pico de Gallo.
- Adjust the spiciness by varying the amount of jalapeño or serrano pepper used. Leave the seeds in for more heat.
- Make sure to taste and adjust the seasoning (lime juice and salt) before serving, as preferences for acidity and saltiness can vary.

Homemade Pico de Gallo is simple to prepare and enhances the freshness and flavor of many dishes with its vibrant ingredients. Enjoy this versatile condiment as a staple in your Mexican-inspired meals!

Grilled Veggie Tacos

Ingredients:

- 1 large bell pepper, sliced into strips
- 1 medium zucchini, sliced lengthwise into strips
- 1 medium yellow squash, sliced lengthwise into strips
- 1 red onion, sliced into rings
- 1 cup cherry tomatoes, halved
- 2 tablespoons olive oil
- 1 teaspoon ground cumin
- 1/2 teaspoon chili powder
- Salt and pepper, to taste
- 8 small corn or flour tortillas
- Optional toppings: sliced avocado, fresh cilantro, salsa, lime wedges

Instructions:

1. **Prepare the Veggies:**
    - Preheat your grill or grill pan over medium-high heat.
    - In a large bowl, toss the bell pepper strips, zucchini, yellow squash, and red onion rings with olive oil, ground cumin, chili powder, salt, and pepper until evenly coated.
2. **Grill the Vegetables:**
    - Place the seasoned vegetables on the preheated grill. Cook for 4-5 minutes per side, or until they are tender and have grill marks. The cooking time may vary depending on the thickness of the vegetables.
3. **Warm the Tortillas:**
    - While the vegetables are grilling, warm the tortillas on the grill for about 30 seconds per side until they are soft and pliable. Alternatively, you can wrap them in foil and warm them in the oven.
4. **Assemble the Tacos:**
    - Once the vegetables are grilled to your liking, remove them from the grill and transfer to a serving platter.
    - Fill each warm tortilla with a generous amount of grilled vegetables.
    - Top with cherry tomatoes, sliced avocado, fresh cilantro, and a squeeze of lime juice if desired.
5. **Serve:**
    - Serve the Grilled Veggie Tacos immediately while warm.

- Offer additional toppings such as salsa, guacamole, or hot sauce on the side.

Tips:

- Feel free to customize the vegetables based on your preference or what you have on hand. Mushrooms, eggplant, or asparagus can also be delicious additions.
- For extra flavor, marinate the vegetables in a mixture of lime juice, garlic, and your favorite herbs before grilling.
- If you prefer softer vegetables, you can steam them briefly before grilling or cook them longer on the grill until they reach the desired texture.

Grilled Veggie Tacos are a nutritious and satisfying meal option that highlights the natural flavors of fresh vegetables. Enjoy the smoky, grilled goodness wrapped in a warm tortilla!

Mexican Corn Salad

Ingredients:

- 4 cups corn kernels (about 4-5 ears of corn)
- 2 tablespoons mayonnaise (or Mexican crema)
- 1-2 tablespoons sour cream (optional)
- Juice of 1 lime
- 1/2 teaspoon chili powder (adjust to taste)
- 1/4 teaspoon cayenne pepper (optional, for heat)
- Salt, to taste
- 1/2 cup cotija cheese, crumbled (or feta cheese)
- 1/4 cup fresh cilantro, chopped
- 2 tablespoons red onion, finely chopped (optional)
- Optional garnish: lime wedges, extra cotija cheese, chopped cilantro

Instructions:

1. **Prepare the Corn:**
    - If using fresh corn on the cob, grill or roast the corn until lightly charred. Alternatively, you can use thawed frozen corn kernels.
    - Cut the kernels off the cob if using fresh corn.
2. **Make the Dressing:**
    - In a small bowl, whisk together mayonnaise (or Mexican crema), sour cream (if using), lime juice, chili powder, cayenne pepper (if using), and salt to taste.
3. **Combine Ingredients:**
    - In a large bowl, combine the grilled or roasted corn kernels with the prepared dressing. Mix well to coat evenly.
4. **Add Cheese and Herbs:**
    - Gently fold in crumbled cotija cheese (or feta cheese), chopped cilantro, and finely chopped red onion (if using). Adjust seasoning if needed.
5. **Chill and Serve:**
    - Cover the bowl with plastic wrap or transfer the Mexican Corn Salad to an airtight container.
    - Refrigerate for at least 30 minutes to allow the flavors to meld together.
6. **Serve:**
    - Serve Mexican Corn Salad (Esquites) chilled or at room temperature.
    - Garnish with extra crumbled cotija cheese, chopped cilantro, and lime wedges on the side.

Tips:

- For a smoky flavor, grill the corn on a barbecue or grill pan until charred. Alternatively, roast it in the oven at high heat.
- Adjust the spiciness by adding more or less chili powder and cayenne pepper according to your preference.
- If you can't find cotija cheese, feta cheese makes a good substitute with a similar crumbly texture and salty flavor.

Mexican Corn Salad (Esquites) is a delightful side dish or appetizer that bursts with fresh flavors and textures. Enjoy its tangy, creamy, and slightly spicy profile as part of your next Mexican-inspired meal or summer gathering!

Black Bean Soup

Ingredients:

- 2 tablespoons olive oil
- 1 onion, chopped
- 2 cloves garlic, minced
- 2 carrots, diced
- 2 stalks celery, diced
- 1 red bell pepper, diced
- 2 teaspoons ground cumin
- 1 teaspoon chili powder (adjust to taste)
- 1 teaspoon smoked paprika
- 1 teaspoon dried oregano
- 4 cups vegetable broth
- 4 cans (15 oz each) black beans, drained and rinsed
- 1 can (14.5 oz) diced tomatoes
- Juice of 1 lime
- Salt and pepper, to taste
- Optional toppings: chopped fresh cilantro, sour cream or Greek yogurt, diced avocado, shredded cheese, tortilla strips

Instructions:

1. **Sauté Aromatics:**
   - In a large pot or Dutch oven, heat olive oil over medium heat.
   - Add chopped onion and cook until softened, about 5 minutes.
   - Stir in minced garlic and cook for another minute until fragrant.
2. **Add Vegetables and Spices:**
   - Add diced carrots, celery, and red bell pepper to the pot. Cook for 5-7 minutes, stirring occasionally, until vegetables begin to soften.
3. **Season and Simmer:**
   - Stir in ground cumin, chili powder, smoked paprika, and dried oregano. Cook for 1-2 minutes to toast the spices.
4. **Add Broth and Beans:**
   - Pour in vegetable broth, drained and rinsed black beans, and diced tomatoes (with their juices). Stir well to combine.
5. **Simmer the Soup:**

- Bring the soup to a boil, then reduce heat to low. Cover and simmer for 20-25 minutes, stirring occasionally, to allow flavors to meld together and vegetables to become tender.

6. **Blend (optional):**
    - For a smoother consistency, use an immersion blender to partially blend the soup directly in the pot. Alternatively, transfer a portion of the soup to a blender and blend until smooth, then return to the pot.

7. **Finish and Serve:**
    - Stir in fresh lime juice.
    - Season with salt and pepper to taste.
    - Serve hot, garnished with optional toppings such as chopped fresh cilantro, a dollop of sour cream or Greek yogurt, diced avocado, shredded cheese, or tortilla strips.

Tips:

- For added protein and texture, you can stir in cooked quinoa, diced tofu, or shredded chicken towards the end of cooking.
- Adjust the thickness of the soup by adding more broth if desired.
- Store leftover soup in an airtight container in the refrigerator for up to 4-5 days or freeze for longer storage.

This Black Bean Soup is comforting, nutritious, and packed with flavors from the blend of spices and vegetables. Enjoy it with your favorite toppings for a satisfying meal!

Jalapeño Poppers

Ingredients:

- 12 fresh jalapeño peppers
- 8 oz cream cheese, softened
- 1 cup shredded cheddar cheese (or your favorite melting cheese)
- 1/2 teaspoon garlic powder
- 1/2 teaspoon onion powder
- 1/4 teaspoon paprika
- Salt and pepper, to taste
- 1 cup breadcrumbs (panko breadcrumbs work well)
- 2 eggs, beaten
- Oil, for frying (if frying)
- Optional: ranch dressing or salsa, for serving

Instructions:

1. **Prepare the Jalapeños:**
   - Wear gloves while handling jalapeños to avoid skin irritation. Slice each jalapeño in half lengthwise and remove the seeds and membranes using a spoon. This step reduces the heat of the peppers.
2. **Make the Filling:**
   - In a mixing bowl, combine softened cream cheese, shredded cheddar cheese, garlic powder, onion powder, paprika, salt, and pepper. Mix until well combined.
3. **Stuff the Jalapeños:**
   - Spoon the cheese mixture into each jalapeño half, filling them evenly.
4. **Bread the Jalapeño Poppers:**
   - Prepare two shallow bowls: one with beaten eggs and another with breadcrumbs.
   - Dip each stuffed jalapeño half into the beaten eggs, coating it completely.
   - Then, roll the jalapeño in breadcrumbs, ensuring it's evenly coated. Press gently to adhere the breadcrumbs.
5. **Fry or Bake the Poppers:**
   - To Fry: Heat oil in a deep skillet or fryer to 350°F (175°C). Fry the breaded jalapeño poppers in batches for 2-3 minutes, or until golden brown and crispy. Remove with a slotted spoon and drain on paper towels.

- To Bake: Preheat your oven to 375°F (190°C). Place the breaded jalapeño poppers on a baking sheet lined with parchment paper. Bake for 15-20 minutes, or until the poppers are golden and the filling is bubbly.

6. **Serve:**
    - Serve the jalapeño poppers hot, optionally with ranch dressing or salsa for dipping.

Tips:

- Adjust the filling's spiciness by adding chopped pickled jalapeños or a dash of hot sauce.
- For a healthier option, bake the jalapeño poppers instead of frying them.
- Experiment with different cheese combinations or add-ins like cooked bacon or diced herbs for variation in flavor.

Jalapeño poppers are best enjoyed fresh and hot, with their crunchy exterior and creamy, cheesy filling providing a delightful contrast in textures and flavors. They make a great appetizer for parties or a fun snack for game day!

Vegetarian Sopes

Ingredients:

- 2 cups masa harina (corn flour)
- 1 1/4 cups warm water
- 1/2 teaspoon salt
- 2 tablespoons vegetable oil, plus more for frying
- 1 cup refried beans
- 1 cup shredded lettuce or cabbage
- 1 cup diced tomatoes
- 1/2 cup crumbled queso fresco or feta cheese
- 1/4 cup chopped fresh cilantro
- Optional toppings: sliced avocado, salsa, sour cream or Mexican crema, pickled jalapeños

Instructions:

1. **Prepare the Sopes Dough:**
    - In a large mixing bowl, combine masa harina and salt. Gradually add warm water and 2 tablespoons of vegetable oil, mixing with your hands until a soft dough forms.
    - Knead the dough for a few minutes until smooth and pliable. If the dough is too dry, add a little more water; if it's too wet, add a little more masa harina.
2. **Form the Sopes:**
    - Divide the dough into 8 equal portions and roll each portion into a ball.
    - Flatten each ball into a disc about 1/4 inch thick. Use your fingers to create a raised edge around the perimeter, forming a small lip to hold the toppings.
3. **Cook the Sopes:**
    - Heat about 1/4 inch of vegetable oil in a large skillet over medium heat.
    - Carefully place the formed sopes in the hot oil, cooking in batches if necessary. Fry each side for about 3-4 minutes, or until golden brown and crispy. Use tongs to flip them halfway through cooking.
    - Remove the sopes from the oil and drain on paper towels.
4. **Assemble the Sopes:**
    - Once the sopes are cooked and cooled slightly, spread a spoonful of refried beans evenly over each one, leaving the raised edges bare.

- Top with shredded lettuce or cabbage, diced tomatoes, crumbled queso fresco or feta cheese, and chopped fresh cilantro.
		- Add any optional toppings you prefer, such as sliced avocado, salsa, sour cream or Mexican crema, and pickled jalapeños.
5. **Serve:**
	- Serve the Vegetarian Sopes immediately while warm.
	- Enjoy as a flavorful and satisfying meal or appetizer.

Tips:

- Customize the toppings based on your preference. You can add grilled or sautéed vegetables, salsa verde, or even a drizzle of chipotle mayo for added flavor.
- If you prefer a healthier option, you can bake the sopes in the oven instead of frying them. Brush them lightly with oil and bake at 400°F (200°C) for about 15-20 minutes until golden and crispy.
- Sopes are best eaten fresh but can be stored in an airtight container in the refrigerator for up to 2 days. Reheat them in the oven to maintain their crispiness.

Vegetarian Sopes are a delicious way to enjoy traditional Mexican flavors in a handheld form. They're perfect for a casual dinner or as part of a festive spread for parties and gatherings.

Red Posole

Ingredients:

- 2 tablespoons vegetable oil
- 1 onion, finely chopped
- 3 cloves garlic, minced
- 2 teaspoons ground cumin
- 1 teaspoon dried oregano
- 1 teaspoon smoked paprika
- 2 dried ancho chilies, stemmed and seeded
- 2 dried guajillo chilies, stemmed and seeded
- 4 cups vegetable broth
- 2 cans (15 oz each) hominy, drained and rinsed
- 1 can (15 oz) diced tomatoes
- 1 cup chopped bell peppers (any color)
- 1 zucchini, diced
- 1 carrot, diced
- Salt and pepper, to taste
- Optional toppings: sliced radishes, shredded cabbage, chopped cilantro, lime wedges, diced avocado, tortilla chips

Instructions:

1. **Prepare the Chilies:**
    - Heat a dry skillet over medium heat. Toast the dried ancho and guajillo chilies for about 1-2 minutes per side until fragrant. Be careful not to burn them.
    - Transfer the toasted chilies to a bowl and cover with hot water. Let them soak for about 20-30 minutes until softened.
2. **Make the Red Chile Sauce:**
    - Once softened, drain the soaked chilies and transfer them to a blender or food processor.
    - Add 1 cup of vegetable broth, minced garlic, ground cumin, dried oregano, and smoked paprika.
    - Blend until smooth, adding more broth if needed to achieve a sauce-like consistency.
3. **Cook the Vegetables:**
    - In a large pot or Dutch oven, heat vegetable oil over medium heat. Add chopped onion and cook until softened, about 5-7 minutes.

- Stir in chopped bell peppers, diced zucchini, and diced carrot. Cook for another 5 minutes until vegetables begin to soften.

4. **Simmer the Posole:**
   - Pour the blended red chile sauce into the pot with the cooked vegetables.
   - Add the remaining vegetable broth, drained hominy, and diced tomatoes (with their juices). Stir well to combine.
   - Bring the posole to a boil, then reduce heat to low. Cover and simmer for 20-25 minutes, stirring occasionally, until the vegetables are tender and the flavors have melded together.

5. **Season and Serve:**
   - Season the Vegetarian Red Posole with salt and pepper to taste.
   - Ladle the posole into bowls and serve hot.
   - Garnish with optional toppings such as sliced radishes, shredded cabbage, chopped cilantro, lime wedges, diced avocado, and tortilla chips.

Tips:

- If you prefer a spicier posole, you can add more dried chilies or include a pinch of cayenne pepper in the sauce.
- For a richer flavor, you can sauté the vegetables in achiote or annatto oil before adding the broth and chile sauce.
- Posole is often served with corn tortillas or cornbread on the side to soak up the delicious broth.

Vegetarian Red Posole is a comforting and flavorful stew that celebrates the richness of Mexican cuisine without meat. It's perfect for a hearty meal on a chilly day or as a centerpiece for gatherings with friends and family. Enjoy the robust flavors and textures of this traditional dish!

Spinach Enchiladas

Ingredients:

- 2 cups fresh spinach, chopped
- 1 small onion, finely chopped
- 2 cloves garlic, minced
- 1 can (15 oz) black beans, drained and rinsed
- 1 teaspoon ground cumin
- 1/2 teaspoon chili powder (adjust to taste)
- Salt and pepper, to taste
- 1 cup shredded cheese (Mexican blend or Monterey Jack), divided
- 10-12 corn tortillas
- 2 cups enchilada sauce (store-bought or homemade)
- Optional toppings: chopped fresh cilantro, sliced jalapeños, diced avocado, sour cream or Mexican crema

Instructions:

1. **Prepare the Filling:**
    - In a large skillet, heat a tablespoon of olive oil over medium heat. Add chopped onion and minced garlic, sautéing until softened and fragrant, about 3-4 minutes.
    - Add chopped spinach to the skillet and cook until wilted, about 2-3 minutes.
    - Stir in black beans, ground cumin, chili powder, salt, and pepper. Cook for another 2-3 minutes until heated through.
    - Remove from heat and stir in 1/2 cup of shredded cheese until melted and combined. Set aside.
2. **Prepare the Tortillas:**
    - Preheat oven to 350°F (175°C). Lightly grease a 9x13-inch baking dish.
    - Warm the corn tortillas in the microwave or on a skillet until soft and pliable. This helps prevent them from breaking when rolled.
3. **Assemble the Enchiladas:**
    - Spoon a generous portion of the spinach and black bean filling onto each tortilla. Roll up tightly and place seam-side down in the prepared baking dish.
    - Repeat with the remaining tortillas and filling, arranging them snugly in the baking dish.
4. **Top with Enchilada Sauce and Cheese:**

- Pour enchilada sauce evenly over the rolled tortillas, covering them completely.
- Sprinkle the remaining 1/2 cup of shredded cheese over the top.

5. **Bake the Enchiladas:**
   - Cover the baking dish with aluminum foil and bake in the preheated oven for 20-25 minutes, until the enchiladas are heated through and the cheese is melted and bubbly.
6. **Serve:**
   - Remove from the oven and let cool slightly before serving.
   - Garnish with chopped fresh cilantro, sliced jalapeños, diced avocado, and a dollop of sour cream or Mexican crema, if desired.

Tips:

- You can customize the filling by adding diced bell peppers, corn kernels, or mushrooms.
- If you prefer a spicier dish, add a dash of hot sauce or more chili powder to the filling.
- Ensure the corn tortillas are warmed before rolling to prevent them from cracking.

These Spinach Enchiladas are packed with flavor and make a satisfying vegetarian meal. They are perfect for family dinners or gatherings, offering a comforting and delicious taste of Mexican cuisine. Enjoy the layers of cheesy goodness and hearty spinach filling in every bite!

Veggie Chilaquiles

Ingredients:

- 1 tablespoon vegetable oil
- 1 onion, finely chopped
- 2 cloves garlic, minced
- 1 bell pepper (any color), diced
- 1 zucchini, diced
- 1 cup corn kernels (fresh or frozen)
- 1 can (15 oz) black beans, drained and rinsed
- 2 cups enchilada sauce (store-bought or homemade)
- 6 cups tortilla chips (thick and sturdy ones work best)
- 1 cup shredded cheese (Mexican blend or Monterey Jack), divided
- Salt and pepper, to taste
- Optional toppings: sliced avocado, chopped fresh cilantro, diced red onion, sour cream or Mexican crema, lime wedges

Instructions:

1. **Sauté the Vegetables:**
    - In a large skillet or frying pan, heat vegetable oil over medium heat.
    - Add chopped onion and sauté until translucent, about 3-4 minutes.
    - Stir in minced garlic and diced bell pepper, cooking for another 2 minutes until the peppers begin to soften.
2. **Add Zucchini, Corn, and Black Beans:**
    - Add diced zucchini and corn kernels to the skillet. Cook for 5-7 minutes, stirring occasionally, until the vegetables are tender.
3. **Simmer with Enchilada Sauce:**
    - Pour enchilada sauce over the sautéed vegetables and stir to combine.
    - Add drained and rinsed black beans to the skillet. Season with salt and pepper to taste.
    - Simmer for 5-7 minutes, allowing the flavors to meld together and the sauce to thicken slightly.
4. **Add Tortilla Chips and Cheese:**
    - Gently fold in tortilla chips, stirring to coat them evenly with the sauce and vegetables. The chips should soften slightly but still retain some texture.
    - Sprinkle half of the shredded cheese over the top and gently stir to incorporate.
5. **Serve:**

- Transfer the Veggie Chilaquiles to a serving platter or individual plates.
- Sprinkle the remaining shredded cheese over the top.
- Garnish with optional toppings such as sliced avocado, chopped fresh cilantro, diced red onion, a dollop of sour cream or Mexican crema, and lime wedges.

Tips:

- If you prefer a spicier dish, add a diced jalapeño or serrano pepper to the sautéed vegetables.
- For a quicker version, you can use store-bought tortilla chips instead of making your own.
- Serve immediately while the tortilla chips are still crispy. Chilaquiles are traditionally enjoyed for breakfast or brunch but make a satisfying meal any time of day.

Veggie Chilaquiles are a versatile dish that can be customized with your favorite vegetables and toppings. Enjoy the layers of flavors and textures in this comforting Mexican-inspired meal!

Bean and Cheese Taquitos

Ingredients:

- 12 small corn tortillas
- 1 can (15 oz) refried beans
- 1 cup shredded cheese (cheddar, Monterey Jack, or Mexican blend)
- 1 teaspoon ground cumin
- 1/2 teaspoon chili powder (optional, for extra flavor)
- Salt and pepper, to taste
- Vegetable oil, for frying
- Optional toppings: salsa, guacamole, sour cream, chopped cilantro, diced tomatoes

Instructions:

1. **Prepare the Filling:**
    - In a mixing bowl, combine refried beans, shredded cheese, ground cumin, chili powder (if using), salt, and pepper. Mix well until all ingredients are evenly incorporated.
2. **Assemble the Taquitos:**
    - Warm the corn tortillas in the microwave or on a skillet until they are soft and pliable.
    - Spoon about 2 tablespoons of the bean and cheese mixture onto each tortilla, spreading it in a line along the center.
3. **Roll the Taquitos:**
    - Roll up each tortilla tightly around the filling to form a taquito. Secure with toothpicks if needed to keep them rolled.
4. **Fry the Taquitos:**
    - In a large skillet, heat about 1/2 inch of vegetable oil over medium-high heat until hot but not smoking.
    - Carefully place the rolled taquitos seam-side down in the hot oil, working in batches to avoid overcrowding the pan.
    - Fry for 2-3 minutes per side, or until golden brown and crispy. Use tongs to turn them gently.
5. **Serve:**
    - Remove the fried taquitos from the oil and drain on paper towels to remove excess oil.
    - Serve hot, optionally with salsa, guacamole, sour cream, chopped cilantro, and diced tomatoes for dipping or topping.

Tips:

- If you prefer a healthier option, you can bake the taquitos instead of frying them. Preheat your oven to 400°F (200°C), place the rolled taquitos on a baking sheet lined with parchment paper, and bake for 15-20 minutes until crispy.
- Customize the filling by adding diced jalapeños, onions, or spices like smoked paprika or cayenne pepper for extra heat.
- Taquitos can be prepared ahead of time and frozen before frying. When ready to cook, thaw them in the refrigerator overnight and fry or bake as directed.

Bean and Cheese Taquitos are a crowd-pleasing dish that's easy to make and incredibly satisfying. Enjoy the crunchy exterior and gooey, cheesy interior of these delicious Mexican-inspired treats!

Mexican Cauliflower Rice

Ingredients:

- 1 medium head of cauliflower, grated or finely chopped into rice-sized pieces
- 2 tablespoons vegetable oil or olive oil
- 1 small onion, finely chopped
- 2 cloves garlic, minced
- 1 red bell pepper, diced
- 1 jalapeño pepper, seeded and minced (optional, for heat)
- 1 teaspoon ground cumin
- 1/2 teaspoon chili powder
- 1/2 teaspoon smoked paprika
- Salt and pepper, to taste
- 1 can (14.5 oz) diced tomatoes, drained
- 1/4 cup chopped fresh cilantro
- Juice of 1 lime

Instructions:

1. **Prepare the Cauliflower Rice:**
   - Rinse the cauliflower head and pat dry. Cut into florets and then grate using a box grater or pulse in a food processor until it resembles rice-sized pieces. Alternatively, you can finely chop the cauliflower florets with a knife.
2. **Cook the Vegetables:**
   - Heat vegetable oil or olive oil in a large skillet over medium heat. Add chopped onion and cook until softened, about 3-4 minutes.
   - Stir in minced garlic, diced red bell pepper, and minced jalapeño (if using). Cook for another 2 minutes until the vegetables are tender.
3. **Add Spices and Cauliflower Rice:**
   - Sprinkle ground cumin, chili powder, smoked paprika, salt, and pepper over the cooked vegetables. Stir to coat the vegetables evenly with the spices.
   - Add the grated or chopped cauliflower rice to the skillet. Cook for 5-7 minutes, stirring frequently, until the cauliflower is tender but still has a slight bite.
4. **Finish and Serve:**
   - Stir in drained diced tomatoes, chopped fresh cilantro, and lime juice. Cook for another 2-3 minutes to heat through and allow flavors to meld.

- Taste and adjust seasoning with salt, pepper, and additional lime juice if desired.
5. **Serve Warm:**
   - Mexican Cauliflower Rice is ready to serve as a flavorful side dish or base for other Mexican-inspired dishes.

Tips:

- Customize the spice level by adjusting the amount of chili powder and jalapeño used.
- Add protein such as cooked black beans, grilled chicken, or tofu to make it a complete meal.
- Freshly grated cauliflower works best for this recipe, but you can also use store-bought cauliflower rice for convenience.

Mexican Cauliflower Rice is a versatile and nutritious dish that's packed with flavor from the spices, vegetables, and fresh herbs. Enjoy it alongside your favorite Mexican mains or as a healthy alternative to traditional rice dishes!

Vegetarian Empanadas

Ingredients:

For the Dough:

- 3 cups all-purpose flour
- 1 teaspoon salt
- 1/2 cup (1 stick) unsalted butter, cold and cut into cubes
- 1 large egg
- 1/2 cup cold water

For the Filling:

- 1 tablespoon olive oil
- 1 onion, finely chopped
- 2 cloves garlic, minced
- 1 bell pepper, diced (any color)
- 1 zucchini, diced
- 1 cup corn kernels (fresh or frozen)
- 1 can (15 oz) black beans, drained and rinsed
- 1 teaspoon ground cumin
- 1/2 teaspoon chili powder
- 1/2 teaspoon paprika
- Salt and pepper, to taste
- 1 cup shredded cheese (cheddar, Monterey Jack, or Mexican blend)
- Optional: chopped fresh cilantro, diced jalapeños, diced tomatoes

Instructions:

1. **Make the Dough:**
    - In a large bowl, combine the flour and salt. Add the cold, cubed butter and use a pastry cutter or your fingers to work the butter into the flour until it resembles coarse crumbs.
    - In a small bowl, whisk together the egg and cold water. Gradually add the egg mixture to the flour mixture, stirring with a fork until the dough starts to come together.
    - Turn the dough out onto a lightly floured surface and knead gently until smooth. Wrap the dough in plastic wrap and refrigerate for at least 30 minutes.
2. **Prepare the Filling:**

- In a large skillet, heat olive oil over medium heat. Add chopped onion and cook until softened, about 3-4 minutes.
- Stir in minced garlic, diced bell pepper, and diced zucchini. Cook for another 3-4 minutes until vegetables begin to soften.
- Add corn kernels and black beans to the skillet. Stir in ground cumin, chili powder, paprika, salt, and pepper. Cook for another 2-3 minutes until heated through.
- Remove from heat and stir in shredded cheese until melted and combined. Optional: add chopped fresh cilantro, diced jalapeños, or diced tomatoes for extra flavor.

3. **Assemble the Empanadas:**
   - Preheat oven to 375°F (190°C). Line baking sheets with parchment paper.
   - On a lightly floured surface, roll out the chilled dough to about 1/8 inch thickness. Use a round cookie cutter or a small bowl to cut out circles (about 4-5 inches in diameter).

4. **Fill and Seal the Empanadas:**
   - Spoon a tablespoon or two of the filling onto one half of each dough circle, leaving a border around the edge.
   - Fold the other half of the dough over the filling to create a half-moon shape. Press the edges together with a fork to seal, or crimp the edges with your fingers to create a decorative edge.

5. **Bake the Empanadas:**
   - Place the filled empanadas on the prepared baking sheets. Brush the tops with a little beaten egg or milk for a golden finish (optional).
   - Bake in the preheated oven for 20-25 minutes, or until the empanadas are golden brown and crispy.

6. **Serve Warm:**
   - Remove from the oven and let cool slightly before serving.
   - Enjoy these Vegetarian Empanadas warm, optionally with salsa, guacamole, or a dollop of sour cream on the side.

Tips:

- Empanadas can also be fried instead of baked for a crispy exterior. Heat vegetable oil in a deep skillet or fryer to 350°F (175°C) and fry each empanada for 2-3 minutes per side until golden brown.
- Make-ahead tip: You can assemble the empanadas ahead of time and refrigerate them until ready to bake or fry.

- Empanadas are versatile; feel free to customize the filling with your favorite vegetables, beans, or cheeses.

These Vegetarian Empanadas are a delightful treat, perfect for parties, picnics, or a flavorful dinner. Enjoy the crispy crust and savory filling in every bite!

Avocado Tacos

Ingredients:

- 4-6 small flour or corn tortillas
- 2 ripe avocados, peeled, pitted, and sliced
- 1 cup cherry tomatoes, halved
- 1/4 cup red onion, thinly sliced
- 1/4 cup fresh cilantro, chopped
- Juice of 1 lime
- Salt and pepper, to taste
- Optional toppings: salsa, sour cream or Mexican crema, shredded lettuce or cabbage, crumbled queso fresco or feta cheese, sliced jalapeños

Instructions:

1. **Prepare the Avocado Mixture:**
    - In a medium bowl, gently toss together sliced avocados, cherry tomatoes, red onion, and chopped cilantro.
    - Squeeze fresh lime juice over the mixture and season with salt and pepper to taste. Toss gently to combine.
2. **Warm the Tortillas:**
    - Heat a dry skillet over medium heat. Warm each tortilla for about 10-15 seconds per side until they are heated through and pliable. Alternatively, you can warm them in a microwave wrapped in a damp paper towel for 20-30 seconds.
3. **Assemble the Tacos:**
    - Spoon the avocado mixture onto each tortilla, dividing evenly.
    - Add any optional toppings you desire, such as salsa, sour cream or Mexican crema, shredded lettuce or cabbage, crumbled queso fresco or feta cheese, and sliced jalapeños.
4. **Serve:**
    - Serve the Avocado Tacos immediately while the tortillas are warm and the avocados are fresh.
    - Enjoy the creamy and refreshing flavors of these simple yet delicious tacos!

Tips:

- For added protein, you can add black beans, grilled tofu, or your favorite meat substitute to the tacos.
- Customize the toppings based on your preference. Avocado tacos are versatile and can accommodate a variety of flavors and textures.
- If you prefer a spicier version, add a dash of hot sauce or finely chopped jalapeños to the avocado mixture.

These Avocado Tacos are perfect for a quick lunch or dinner, and they make a great option for vegetarian and vegan diets. Enjoy the creamy avocado combined with fresh vegetables and zesty lime juice wrapped in warm tortillas!

Lentil Tacos

Ingredients:

- 1 cup dried lentils (green or brown), rinsed
- 2 cups vegetable broth or water
- 1 tablespoon olive oil
- 1 onion, finely chopped
- 3 cloves garlic, minced
- 1 tablespoon chili powder
- 1 teaspoon ground cumin
- 1/2 teaspoon smoked paprika
- 1/2 teaspoon dried oregano
- Salt and pepper, to taste
- 1 can (15 oz) diced tomatoes
- Juice of 1 lime
- 8-10 small corn or flour tortillas
- Optional toppings: shredded lettuce or cabbage, diced tomatoes, chopped cilantro, sliced jalapeños, salsa, guacamole, sour cream or Mexican crema, shredded cheese

Instructions:

1. **Cook the Lentils:**
    - In a medium saucepan, combine the rinsed lentils and vegetable broth (or water). Bring to a boil over high heat.
    - Reduce heat to low, cover, and simmer for 20-25 minutes, or until lentils are tender and most of the liquid is absorbed. Drain any excess liquid and set aside.
2. **Prepare the Lentil Filling:**
    - In a large skillet, heat olive oil over medium heat. Add chopped onion and cook until softened, about 5-7 minutes.
    - Stir in minced garlic, chili powder, ground cumin, smoked paprika, dried oregano, salt, and pepper. Cook for another 1-2 minutes until fragrant.
3. **Combine with Tomatoes and Lentils:**
    - Add the diced tomatoes (with their juices) to the skillet. Stir to combine with the onion and spice mixture.
    - Add the cooked lentils to the skillet and stir well to coat them with the tomato mixture. Cook for 5-7 minutes, stirring occasionally, until heated through and flavors are blended.

- Remove from heat and squeeze fresh lime juice over the lentil mixture. Taste and adjust seasoning as needed.
4. **Warm the Tortillas:**
   - Heat the tortillas in a dry skillet over medium heat, flipping once, until warmed through and slightly charred. Alternatively, wrap them in a damp paper towel and microwave for 20-30 seconds.
5. **Assemble the Tacos:**
   - Spoon the lentil mixture onto each warm tortilla, dividing evenly.
   - Add your favorite toppings such as shredded lettuce or cabbage, diced tomatoes, chopped cilantro, sliced jalapeños, salsa, guacamole, sour cream or Mexican crema, and shredded cheese.
6. **Serve:**
   - Serve the Lentil Tacos immediately, allowing everyone to customize their tacos with their preferred toppings.
   - Enjoy the delicious and nutritious flavors of these hearty lentil tacos!

Tips:

- You can customize the lentil filling by adding diced bell peppers, corn kernels, or black beans for extra texture and flavor.
- Make-ahead tip: Cook the lentil filling ahead of time and store it in the refrigerator for up to 3 days. Reheat before assembling tacos.
- For a spicier version, add a pinch of cayenne pepper or chopped jalapeños to the lentil mixture.

These Lentil Tacos are a fantastic vegetarian option that satisfies with their robust flavors and wholesome ingredients. They are perfect for a weeknight meal or for entertaining guests who appreciate a delicious and healthy taco experience!

Nopalitos Salad

Ingredients:

- 2-3 fresh nopales (cactus paddles)
- 1 tablespoon olive oil
- 1 small red onion, thinly sliced
- 2 tomatoes, diced
- 1 jalapeño or serrano pepper, seeded and finely chopped (optional, for heat)
- 1/4 cup chopped fresh cilantro
- Juice of 2-3 limes
- Salt and pepper, to taste
- Crumbled queso fresco or feta cheese, for garnish (optional)

Instructions:

1. **Prepare the Nopales:**
   - Using tongs, hold each nopal over an open flame (gas stove or grill) and cook, turning occasionally, until tender and slightly charred, about 5-7 minutes. Alternatively, you can blanch nopales in boiling water for 5 minutes.
   - Rinse the cooked nopales under cold water to cool them down. Pat dry with paper towels and dice into small pieces.
2. **Combine Ingredients:**
   - In a large bowl, combine diced nopales, thinly sliced red onion, diced tomatoes, and chopped jalapeño or serrano pepper (if using).
   - Add chopped fresh cilantro to the bowl.
3. **Season the Salad:**
   - Drizzle olive oil and lime juice over the salad ingredients. Season with salt and pepper to taste.
   - Toss gently to combine, ensuring the nopales are coated evenly with the dressing.
4. **Chill and Serve:**
   - Cover the bowl with plastic wrap or transfer the salad to a serving dish. Refrigerate for at least 30 minutes to allow flavors to meld together.
5. **Garnish and Serve:**
   - Before serving, sprinkle crumbled queso fresco or feta cheese over the top of the salad for added flavor and texture.
   - Serve chilled as a refreshing side dish or as a topping for tacos, tostadas, or grilled meats.

Tips:

- When handling nopales, be cautious of their fine spines. Use tongs to hold them over the flame or wear gloves when cleaning and preparing them.
- Adjust the amount of jalapeño or serrano pepper according to your spice preference. You can also remove the seeds for a milder flavor.
- Nopalitos salad is best served chilled or at room temperature. Allow it to sit for at least 30 minutes before serving to enhance the flavors.

This Nopalitos Salad is a delightful way to enjoy the unique flavor and texture of nopales, complemented by fresh vegetables and zesty lime juice. It makes a perfect addition to any Mexican-inspired meal or as a light and healthy dish on its own.

Veggie Tamale Pie

Ingredients:

For the Filling:

- 1 tablespoon olive oil
- 1 onion, finely chopped
- 2 cloves garlic, minced
- 1 bell pepper (any color), diced
- 1 zucchini, diced
- 1 cup corn kernels (fresh or frozen)
- 1 can (15 oz) black beans, drained and rinsed
- 1 teaspoon ground cumin
- 1/2 teaspoon chili powder
- 1/2 teaspoon smoked paprika
- Salt and pepper, to taste
- 1 can (14.5 oz) diced tomatoes

For the Cornbread Topping:

- 1 cup cornmeal
- 1 cup all-purpose flour
- 1 tablespoon baking powder
- 1/2 teaspoon salt
- 1 cup milk or non-dairy milk
- 1/4 cup vegetable oil
- 1 tablespoon honey or maple syrup (optional)
- 1 egg (or flaxseed egg for vegan option)

Optional Garnishes:

- Sliced jalapeños
- Chopped cilantro
- Sliced avocado
- Sour cream or Mexican crema

Instructions:

1. **Prepare the Filling:**

- In a large skillet, heat olive oil over medium heat. Add chopped onion and cook until softened, about 3-4 minutes.
- Stir in minced garlic and diced bell pepper, cooking for another 2 minutes until peppers begin to soften.
- Add diced zucchini and corn kernels to the skillet. Cook for 5-7 minutes, stirring occasionally, until vegetables are tender.
- Stir in drained black beans, ground cumin, chili powder, smoked paprika, salt, and pepper. Cook for another 2 minutes.
- Pour in diced tomatoes with their juices. Simmer for 5-7 minutes, stirring occasionally, until the mixture thickens slightly. Remove from heat and set aside.

2. **Prepare the Cornbread Topping:**
   - In a mixing bowl, whisk together cornmeal, all-purpose flour, baking powder, and salt.
   - In a separate bowl, whisk together milk, vegetable oil, honey or maple syrup (if using), and egg (or flaxseed egg).
   - Pour the wet ingredients into the dry ingredients and stir until just combined. Do not overmix.

3. **Assemble and Bake:**
   - Preheat your oven to 375°F (190°C). Lightly grease a 9x9-inch baking dish or similar size.
   - Spread the prepared veggie filling evenly into the bottom of the baking dish.
   - Spoon the cornbread batter over the top of the veggie filling, spreading it evenly with a spatula.

4. **Bake the Tamale Pie:**
   - Place the baking dish in the preheated oven and bake for 25-30 minutes, or until the cornbread topping is golden brown and cooked through.

5. **Serve:**
   - Remove from the oven and let the tamale pie cool slightly before serving.
   - Garnish with sliced jalapeños, chopped cilantro, sliced avocado, and a dollop of sour cream or Mexican crema, if desired.

Tips:

- Customize the filling with your favorite vegetables or add diced jalapeños for extra heat.
- Make it vegan by using a flaxseed egg (1 tablespoon ground flaxseed + 3 tablespoons water) in place of the egg and opting for non-dairy milk.

- Leftovers can be stored in an airtight container in the refrigerator for up to 3 days. Reheat in the oven or microwave before serving.

This Veggie Tamale Pie is a comforting and satisfying dish that combines the flavors of a classic tamale with a delicious cornbread topping. It's perfect for a family dinner or potluck, offering a wholesome meal that everyone will enjoy!

Roasted Tomatillo Salsa

Ingredients:

- 1 lb tomatillos, husked and rinsed
- 1-2 jalapeño peppers (adjust to taste), stemmed and halved
- 1/2 cup chopped white onion
- 2 cloves garlic, peeled
- 1/4 cup chopped fresh cilantro
- Juice of 1 lime
- Salt, to taste

Instructions:

1. **Roast the Tomatillos and Peppers:**
   - Preheat your broiler (oven grill) to high. Place the tomatillos and jalapeño peppers on a baking sheet lined with aluminum foil.
   - Broil for 5-7 minutes, turning halfway through, until the tomatillos and peppers are charred and softened. Alternatively, you can roast them on a hot grill or directly over a gas flame until charred.
2. **Prepare the Salsa:**
   - Once roasted, transfer the tomatillos, jalapeños, and any juices from the baking sheet into a blender or food processor.
   - Add chopped white onion, garlic cloves, chopped cilantro, and lime juice to the blender or food processor.
3. **Blend Until Smooth:**
   - Blend all the ingredients until smooth. If you prefer a chunkier salsa, pulse a few times until you reach your desired consistency. Taste and adjust salt as needed.
4. **Chill and Serve:**
   - Transfer the salsa verde to a bowl or airtight container. Refrigerate for at least 30 minutes to allow the flavors to meld together.
5. **Serve:**
   - Serve the Roasted Tomatillo Salsa chilled or at room temperature.
   - Enjoy with tortilla chips, as a topping for tacos, enchiladas, or any of your favorite Mexican dishes.

Tips:

- If you prefer a milder salsa, remove the seeds and membranes from the jalapeño peppers before roasting.
- Customize the salsa by adding other ingredients like avocado or roasted garlic for added depth of flavor.
- Store leftover salsa verde in an airtight container in the refrigerator for up to one week.

Roasted Tomatillo Salsa (Salsa Verde) adds a bright and zesty flavor to your meals, enhancing the dish with its tangy and slightly smoky notes. It's a versatile condiment that complements a wide range of dishes, making it a staple in Mexican cuisine. Enjoy the fresh flavors of this homemade salsa verde!

Vegetarian Frito Pie

Ingredients:

- 1 tablespoon olive oil
- 1 onion, diced
- 2 cloves garlic, minced
- 1 bell pepper (any color), diced
- 1 zucchini, diced
- 1 can (15 oz) black beans, drained and rinsed
- 1 can (15 oz) diced tomatoes
- 1 cup corn kernels (fresh or frozen)
- 1 teaspoon ground cumin
- 1 teaspoon chili powder
- 1/2 teaspoon smoked paprika
- Salt and pepper, to taste
- 1 bag (9.25 oz) Fritos corn chips (or similar)
- 1 cup shredded cheese (cheddar, Monterey Jack, or Mexican blend)
- Optional toppings: sliced jalapeños, diced red onion, chopped cilantro, sour cream or Greek yogurt, avocado slices, salsa

Instructions:

1. **Prepare the Vegetarian Chili Mixture:**
   - In a large skillet, heat olive oil over medium heat. Add diced onion and cook until softened, about 5 minutes.
   - Stir in minced garlic and diced bell pepper. Cook for another 3-4 minutes until peppers begin to soften.
   - Add diced zucchini, black beans, diced tomatoes (with juices), and corn kernels to the skillet. Stir in ground cumin, chili powder, smoked paprika, salt, and pepper. Cook for 10-12 minutes, stirring occasionally, until vegetables are tender and the mixture has thickened slightly.
2. **Assemble the Frito Pie:**
   - Preheat your oven to 350°F (175°C).
   - Arrange half of the Fritos corn chips in an even layer on the bottom of a baking dish or a large oven-safe skillet.
   - Spoon half of the vegetarian chili mixture evenly over the Fritos layer.
   - Sprinkle half of the shredded cheese over the chili mixture.
   - Repeat with another layer of Fritos, followed by the remaining chili mixture, and top with the remaining shredded cheese.

3. **Bake the Frito Pie:**
   - Place the assembled Frito Pie in the preheated oven and bake for 15-20 minutes, or until the cheese is melted and bubbly.
4. **Serve:**
   - Remove from the oven and let cool slightly before serving.
   - Garnish with optional toppings such as sliced jalapeños, diced red onion, chopped cilantro, sour cream or Greek yogurt, avocado slices, and salsa.

Tips:

- Customize the chili mixture with your favorite vegetables or add a variety of beans like kidney beans or pinto beans.
- For a spicier Frito Pie, add additional chili powder, cayenne pepper, or hot sauce to taste.
- Make it vegan by omitting the cheese or using a vegan cheese alternative.

This Vegetarian Frito Pie is a satisfying and flavorful dish that's perfect for a casual dinner or game day snack. Enjoy the crunchy Fritos combined with the hearty vegetarian chili and your favorite toppings for a Tex-Mex treat!

Chipotle Sweet Potato Tacos

Ingredients:

- 2 large sweet potatoes, peeled and diced into small cubes
- 2 tablespoons olive oil
- 1-2 chipotle peppers in adobo sauce, minced (adjust to taste)
- 1 teaspoon adobo sauce (from the can of chipotle peppers)
- 1 teaspoon ground cumin
- 1/2 teaspoon smoked paprika
- Salt and pepper, to taste
- 8-10 small corn or flour tortillas
- Optional toppings: shredded lettuce or cabbage, diced avocado, chopped cilantro, crumbled queso fresco or feta cheese, lime wedges

Instructions:

1. **Roast the Sweet Potatoes:**
    - Preheat your oven to 400°F (200°C).
    - In a large bowl, toss the diced sweet potatoes with olive oil, minced chipotle peppers, adobo sauce, ground cumin, smoked paprika, salt, and pepper until evenly coated.
    - Spread the sweet potatoes in a single layer on a baking sheet lined with parchment paper or aluminum foil.
    - Roast in the preheated oven for 20-25 minutes, stirring halfway through, until the sweet potatoes are tender and lightly caramelized.
2. **Prepare the Tortillas:**
    - While the sweet potatoes are roasting, heat the tortillas in a dry skillet over medium heat, flipping each tortilla for about 10-15 seconds per side until they are warmed through and pliable. Alternatively, warm them in a microwave wrapped in a damp paper towel for 20-30 seconds.
3. **Assemble the Tacos:**
    - Spoon the roasted chipotle sweet potatoes onto each warm tortilla.
    - Add optional toppings such as shredded lettuce or cabbage, diced avocado, chopped cilantro, and crumbled queso fresco or feta cheese.
4. **Serve:**
    - Serve the Chipotle Sweet Potato Tacos warm, with lime wedges on the side for squeezing over the tacos.

Tips:

- For added protein, you can add black beans, grilled tofu, or your favorite meat substitute to the tacos.
- Adjust the amount of chipotle peppers and adobo sauce according to your spice preference. Start with less and add more for extra heat.
- Customize the toppings based on your preference. These tacos are versatile and can accommodate a variety of flavors and textures.

These Chipotle Sweet Potato Tacos are a delicious and satisfying vegetarian option that highlights the smoky and spicy flavors of chipotle peppers combined with the sweetness of roasted sweet potatoes. Enjoy these tacos for a flavorful meal that's perfect for any occasion!

Mexican Grilled Corn Salad (Esquites)

Ingredients:

- 4 ears of corn, husked
- 2 tablespoons mayonnaise
- 2 tablespoons sour cream or Mexican crema
- 1/2 cup crumbled cotija cheese or feta cheese
- 1/4 cup chopped fresh cilantro
- 1 jalapeño pepper, seeded and finely chopped (optional, for heat)
- 1 clove garlic, minced
- Juice of 1 lime
- 1/2 teaspoon chili powder (such as ancho or chipotle)
- Salt, to taste
- Tortilla chips or tostadas, for serving (optional)

Instructions:

1. **Grill the Corn:**
    - Preheat your grill to medium-high heat. Grill the ears of corn, turning occasionally, until lightly charred on all sides, about 10-12 minutes in total.
    - Alternatively, you can cook the corn on a stovetop grill pan or boil them in water for 5-7 minutes. Let the corn cool slightly before proceeding.
2. **Prepare the Salad:**
    - Once the corn is cool enough to handle, cut the kernels off the cobs using a sharp knife. Place the kernels in a large mixing bowl.
3. **Mix the Dressing:**
    - In a small bowl, whisk together mayonnaise, sour cream or Mexican crema, crumbled cotija cheese or feta cheese, chopped cilantro, finely chopped jalapeño (if using), minced garlic, lime juice, chili powder, and salt.
4. **Combine and Chill:**
    - Pour the dressing over the grilled corn kernels in the large mixing bowl. Gently toss until the corn is evenly coated with the dressing.
5. **Serve:**
    - Serve the Mexican Grilled Corn Salad (Esquites) in individual bowls or cups.
    - Optionally, serve with tortilla chips or tostadas for scooping up the salad.

Tips:

- Adjust the amount of jalapeño and chili powder according to your spice preference.
- If cotija cheese is unavailable, feta cheese makes a good substitute for its crumbly texture and salty flavor.
- Esquites is traditionally served warm or at room temperature, but it can also be chilled for a refreshing twist.

This Mexican Grilled Corn Salad (Esquites) is bursting with flavors from the grilled corn, creamy dressing, and zesty lime juice, making it a perfect side dish or appetizer for any Mexican-inspired meal or barbecue. Enjoy the delicious combination of textures and tastes!

Roasted Pepper Quesadillas

Ingredients:

- 2 large bell peppers (any color), roasted, peeled, seeded, and thinly sliced
- 4 large flour tortillas (burrito size)
- 2 cups shredded cheese (such as Monterey Jack, cheddar, or a Mexican blend)
- 1 tablespoon olive oil or butter, for cooking
- Optional toppings: sour cream, salsa, guacamole, chopped cilantro

Instructions:

1. **Roast and Prepare the Peppers:**
   - Preheat your broiler (oven grill) to high. Place whole bell peppers on a baking sheet lined with aluminum foil.
   - Broil the peppers, turning occasionally, until the skins are charred and blistered on all sides, about 10-15 minutes.
   - Transfer the roasted peppers to a bowl and cover with plastic wrap. Let them steam for 10 minutes to loosen the skins.
   - Peel off the skins, remove the seeds and stems, and thinly slice the roasted peppers.
2. **Assemble the Quesadillas:**
   - Heat a large skillet or griddle over medium heat.
   - Place one tortilla in the skillet. Sprinkle 1/2 cup of shredded cheese evenly over the tortilla.
   - Arrange a layer of sliced roasted peppers evenly over the cheese.
   - Top with another 1/2 cup of shredded cheese.
   - Place another tortilla on top to cover the filling.
3. **Cook the Quesadillas:**
   - Cook the quesadilla for 3-4 minutes on each side, or until the tortillas are golden brown and crispy, and the cheese is melted.
   - Repeat the process with the remaining tortillas and filling ingredients.
4. **Serve:**
   - Remove the quesadillas from the skillet and let them cool for a minute before cutting them into wedges.
   - Serve hot, with optional toppings such as sour cream, salsa, guacamole, or chopped cilantro.

Tips:

- Customize your quesadillas by adding other ingredients like sliced onions, black beans, or jalapeños.
- For a quicker option, you can use store-bought roasted peppers in a jar, drained and sliced.
- Make it spicy by adding a sprinkle of chili flakes or hot sauce before cooking.

These Roasted Pepper Quesadillas are perfect for a quick lunch, dinner, or snack. They're crispy on the outside, cheesy on the inside, and packed with the delicious flavor of roasted peppers. Enjoy this simple and satisfying dish!

Mexican Black Bean Salad

Ingredients:

- 2 cups cooked black beans (or 1 can, drained and rinsed)
- 1 cup corn kernels (fresh or thawed if frozen)
- 1 red bell pepper, diced
- 1/2 red onion, finely chopped
- 1 jalapeño, seeded and finely chopped (optional, for heat)
- 1/4 cup chopped fresh cilantro
- Juice of 2 limes
- 2 tablespoons olive oil
- 1 teaspoon ground cumin
- 1/2 teaspoon chili powder
- Salt and pepper, to taste
- Optional toppings: diced avocado, crumbled feta or cotija cheese, sliced black olives, chopped green onions

Instructions:

1. **Prepare the Dressing:**
    - In a small bowl, whisk together the lime juice, olive oil, ground cumin, chili powder, salt, and pepper. Set aside.
2. **Assemble the Salad:**
    - In a large mixing bowl, combine the cooked black beans, corn kernels, diced red bell pepper, finely chopped red onion, jalapeño (if using), and chopped cilantro.
3. **Add the Dressing:**
    - Pour the prepared dressing over the salad ingredients in the bowl.
    - Toss gently to coat everything evenly with the dressing.
4. **Chill and Serve:**
    - Cover the bowl with plastic wrap or transfer the salad to an airtight container.
    - Refrigerate for at least 30 minutes to allow the flavors to meld together.
5. **Serve:**
    - Before serving, toss the salad again to redistribute the dressing.
    - Serve chilled, topped with optional toppings such as diced avocado, crumbled feta or cotija cheese, sliced black olives, and chopped green onions.

Tips:

- If you prefer a milder salad, you can omit the jalapeño or adjust the amount according to your spice preference.
- Customize the salad by adding other ingredients like cherry tomatoes, diced cucumber, or bell peppers of different colors.
- This salad can be served as a side dish, a topping for tacos or quesadillas, or enjoyed on its own as a light and nutritious meal.

This Mexican Black Bean Salad is refreshing, nutritious, and packed with flavors that complement each other perfectly. It's a great dish for picnics, potlucks, or any occasion where you want to enjoy a taste of Mexican-inspired cuisine!

Cauliflower Tacos

Ingredients:

- 1 medium head of cauliflower, cut into small florets
- 2 tablespoons olive oil
- 1 teaspoon chili powder
- 1/2 teaspoon ground cumin
- 1/2 teaspoon smoked paprika
- 1/2 teaspoon garlic powder
- Salt and pepper, to taste
- 8-10 small corn or flour tortillas
- Optional toppings: shredded lettuce or cabbage, diced avocado, chopped cilantro, lime wedges, salsa, sour cream or Greek yogurt (for non-vegan)

Instructions:

1. **Prepare the Cauliflower:**
   - Preheat your oven to 425°F (220°C).
   - In a large bowl, toss the cauliflower florets with olive oil, chili powder, ground cumin, smoked paprika, garlic powder, salt, and pepper until evenly coated.
   - Spread the seasoned cauliflower in a single layer on a baking sheet lined with parchment paper.
2. **Roast the Cauliflower:**
   - Roast in the preheated oven for 20-25 minutes, stirring halfway through, until the cauliflower is tender and caramelized on the edges.
3. **Warm the Tortillas:**
   - While the cauliflower is roasting, warm the tortillas in a dry skillet over medium heat, flipping each tortilla for about 10-15 seconds per side until they are warmed through and pliable. Alternatively, warm them in a microwave wrapped in a damp paper towel for 20-30 seconds.
4. **Assemble the Tacos:**
   - Fill each tortilla with a generous amount of roasted cauliflower florets.
   - Add optional toppings such as shredded lettuce or cabbage, diced avocado, chopped cilantro, and a squeeze of lime juice.
5. **Serve:**
   - Serve the Cauliflower Tacos warm, with additional toppings and your favorite salsa or sauce.

Tips:

- Customize your cauliflower tacos with additional toppings like sliced radishes, pickled red onions, or a drizzle of chipotle sauce.
- For a vegan option, use non-dairy yogurt or skip the sour cream.
- Make it spicy by adding sliced jalapeños or a sprinkle of cayenne pepper to the cauliflower seasoning mixture before roasting.

These Cauliflower Tacos are a delicious and healthy alternative to traditional meat-based tacos. They're packed with flavor, easy to make, and perfect for a quick weeknight dinner or a fun taco night with family and friends. Enjoy the tasty combination of roasted cauliflower and fresh toppings in every bite!

Vegan Taco Salad

Ingredients:

For the Salad:

- 1 can (15 oz) black beans, drained and rinsed
- 1 cup corn kernels (fresh or thawed if frozen)
- 1 cup cherry tomatoes, halved
- 1/2 red onion, thinly sliced
- 1 avocado, diced
- 1/4 cup chopped cilantro
- 4 cups mixed greens (such as lettuce, spinach, or arugula)
- Optional: sliced jalapeños, diced bell peppers, shredded carrots

For the Dressing:

- 1/4 cup olive oil
- Juice of 1 lime
- 2 tablespoons chopped fresh cilantro
- 1 teaspoon ground cumin
- 1/2 teaspoon chili powder
- Salt and pepper, to taste

Optional Toppings:

- Tortilla strips or crushed tortilla chips
- Sliced black olives
- Salsa or pico de gallo
- Guacamole or diced avocado

Instructions:

1. **Prepare the Dressing:**
    - In a small bowl, whisk together olive oil, lime juice, chopped cilantro, ground cumin, chili powder, salt, and pepper. Set aside.
2. **Assemble the Salad:**
    - In a large mixing bowl, combine the drained and rinsed black beans, corn kernels, cherry tomatoes, thinly sliced red onion, diced avocado, and chopped cilantro.
    - Add the mixed greens to the bowl.

3. **Add the Dressing:**
    - Pour the prepared dressing over the salad ingredients in the bowl.
    - Toss gently to coat everything evenly with the dressing.
4. **Serve:**
    - Divide the Vegan Taco Salad among serving plates or bowls.
    - Top each serving with optional toppings such as tortilla strips or crushed tortilla chips, sliced black olives, salsa or pico de gallo, and guacamole or diced avocado.
5. **Enjoy:**
    - Serve immediately and enjoy this fresh and flavorful Vegan Taco Salad!

Tips:

- Customize your Vegan Taco Salad with additional toppings like shredded vegan cheese, diced bell peppers, or your favorite vegan protein such as marinated tofu or tempeh.
- For added protein, you can also add quinoa or cooked lentils to the salad.
- Make the dressing ahead of time and store it in the refrigerator until ready to use. Give it a good stir before adding to the salad.

This Vegan Taco Salad is packed with nutritious ingredients, vibrant colors, and bold flavors that will satisfy your taco cravings while providing a wholesome and satisfying meal. It's perfect for lunch, dinner, or even as a crowd-pleasing dish for potlucks and parties!

Veggie Stuffed Avocados

Ingredients:

- 2 ripe avocados
- 1 cup cherry tomatoes, quartered
- 1/2 cup cucumber, diced
- 1/2 cup bell pepper (any color), diced
- 1/4 cup red onion, finely chopped
- 1/4 cup fresh cilantro, chopped
- Juice of 1 lime
- 2 tablespoons olive oil
- Salt and pepper, to taste
- Optional: diced jalapeño for spice, crumbled feta or cotija cheese for garnish

Instructions:

1. **Prepare the Avocados:**
    - Cut the avocados in half lengthwise and remove the pits. Scoop out a little bit of flesh from each half to create a larger cavity for the filling, leaving a border around the edges.
2. **Prepare the Veggie Mixture:**
    - In a bowl, combine the quartered cherry tomatoes, diced cucumber, diced bell pepper, finely chopped red onion, and chopped cilantro.
3. **Make the Dressing:**
    - In a small bowl, whisk together the lime juice, olive oil, salt, and pepper.
4. **Combine and Stuff the Avocados:**
    - Pour the dressing over the veggie mixture and toss gently to coat.
    - Spoon the veggie mixture into the hollowed-out avocados, filling each avocado half generously.
5. **Serve:**
    - Optional: Garnish with diced jalapeño for added spice and crumbled feta or cotija cheese for extra flavor.
    - Serve immediately and enjoy these Veggie Stuffed Avocados as a light and refreshing appetizer or a healthy snack.

Tips:

- You can customize the veggie mixture based on your preference. Add ingredients like corn, black beans, or diced mango for additional flavors and textures.

- For a creamy texture, mash some of the avocado flesh and mix it with the veggie mixture before filling the avocado halves.
- Serve Veggie Stuffed Avocados immediately to prevent them from browning, or drizzle extra lime juice over the avocados to help preserve their color.

This Veggie Stuffed Avocados recipe is quick to prepare, full of fresh flavors, and makes for a beautiful presentation. It's perfect for a light lunch or as a side dish alongside your favorite main course. Enjoy the creamy avocado paired with the crisp and colorful veggie filling!

Mexican Chocolate Avocado Mousse

Ingredients:

- 2 ripe avocados, peeled and pitted
- 1/2 cup unsweetened cocoa powder
- 1/2 cup maple syrup or agave nectar (adjust to taste)
- 1 teaspoon vanilla extract
- 1/2 teaspoon ground cinnamon
- 1/4 teaspoon ground nutmeg
- Pinch of cayenne pepper (optional, for a hint of spice)
- Pinch of salt
- Fresh berries, for garnish (optional)

Instructions:

1. **Prepare the Avocados:**
   - Scoop the flesh of the ripe avocados into a food processor or blender.
2. **Blend the Mousse:**
   - Add the unsweetened cocoa powder, maple syrup or agave nectar, vanilla extract, ground cinnamon, ground nutmeg, cayenne pepper (if using), and a pinch of salt to the avocados.
   - Blend until smooth and creamy, scraping down the sides of the processor or blender as needed to ensure everything is well combined.
3. **Chill (optional):**
   - For a firmer texture, transfer the chocolate avocado mixture to a bowl and refrigerate for at least 30 minutes before serving.
4. **Serve:**
   - Spoon the Mexican Chocolate Avocado Mousse into serving bowls or glasses.
   - Garnish with fresh berries or any topping of your choice, such as chopped nuts, shredded coconut, or a sprinkle of cocoa powder.
5. **Enjoy:**
   - Serve immediately and enjoy this indulgent Mexican Chocolate Avocado Mousse as a satisfying dessert or a guilt-free treat!

Tips:

- Adjust the sweetness by adding more or less maple syrup or agave nectar according to your preference.

- If you prefer a smoother texture, blend the mixture for a longer period of time.
- The pinch of cayenne pepper adds a subtle kick to the mousse, which complements the richness of the chocolate. Adjust the amount according to your taste preference.

This Mexican Chocolate Avocado Mousse is not only delicious but also packed with nutritious ingredients like avocados and cocoa powder. It's a perfect dessert for those who enjoy a balance of flavors and a creamy, decadent texture. Enjoy this delightful treat on its own or as a finishing touch to any meal!

www.ingramcontent.com/pod-product-compliance
Lightning Source LLC
LaVergne TN
LVHW081559060526
838201LV00054B/1967